KEYS TO ISRAEL

Unlocking the Truth to God's Holy Land

RABBI YECHIEL ECKSTEIN

FOREWORD BY YAEL ECKSTEIN

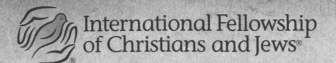
International Fellowship
of Christians and Jews®

KEYS TO
ISRAEL

Unlocking the Truth to God's Holy Land

RABBI YECHIEL ECKSTEIN

FOREWORD BY YAEL ECKSTEIN

Keys to Israel —
Unlocking the Truth to God's Holy Land

Unless otherwise noted, all quotations are taken from
the *Holy Bible, New International Version®*, NIV®.
Copyright © 1973, 1978, 1984, 2011 by Biblica, Inc.™
Used by permission. All rights reserved worldwide.

Cover and interior design by **Design Corps**,
Colorado Springs, CO (designcorps.us)
IFCJ Project Staff: Caleb Burroughs, George Mamo,
Yonit Rothchild, and Betsy Schmitt.

Published by the International Fellowship of
Christians & Jews, Inc. with offices in Canada, Israel,
South Korea, and the United States.

ISBN 978-0-9835327-5-0

First printing: 2018

IMAGES CREDITS

Cover:

iStockphoto:
Golden Gate (photography by AndreyCrav)
Keys on ring (photography by mofles)

Interior:

AllFreeDownload.com: pages xii, 28, 107
& 112

Bible Picture Gallery: page 39

The Brooklyn Museum: pages 74, 134 & 140

Creationism.org: page 160

Deposit Photos: pages 34, 42, 48, 150 & 151(4x)

IFCJ: pages vi, vii, ix, x, xi, 3, 7, 50, 77, 78, 88,
89, 92, 93, 103, 104, 110, 147, 152, 153, 155 & 161

Isranet: page 18

iStockphoto: pages 10, 14, 16, 20, 23, 24, 36,
48 & 49(3x), 79, 124, 126, 144 & 146

JewishEncyclopedia.com: page 43

The Jewish Museum: pages 38, 58, 108 &
109(3x), 120 & 138

Palmach Museum: page 55

Shutterstock: pages 22, 32, 44, 46, 54, 64, 65,
68, 76, 80, 81, 84, 94, 95, 99, 122, 142, 143, 148,
149, 152, 156 & 158

Wikimedia: pages viii, 1, 2, 4, 8, 9, 12, 13, 15,
17, 19, 21, 25, 26(2x), 27, 29, 30, 33, 36, 40, 45,
46, 51, 52, 55, 56(2x), 59, 60, 62, 63, 66(2x), 69,
70(2x), 72, 73, 82, 83, 84 & 85(6x), 86, 87, 90,
91, 96, 98, 100, 100 & 101(3x), 102, 105, 106,
111, 113, 114, 115, 116, 117, 118, 121, 125, 127,
128, 130, 131, 132, 133, 135, 136, 137 & 154

TABLE OF CONTENTS

FOREWORD

I was raised on the words of Psalm 90:12: *"Teach us to number our days, that we may gain a heart of wisdom."* Life is too short to waste our precious time here on earth. I was taught to make the most of the time given to me in order to maximize my potential and contribution to the world. While it is true that no one has enough time to fix everything, if we are willing to work hard and consistently, each of us has the ability to contribute something.

Rabbi Yechiel Eckstein and Yael Eckstein in Jerusalem (IFCJ)

That desire and legacy was passed down to me by my mother, and also by my father, Rabbi Yechiel Eckstein. It has shaped my life in ways I never felt possible. It has been a journey that, in many ways, has paralleled the journey of my own people during the past 70 years.

As I look back on the last 70 years since the establishment of the state of Israel, it seems that Israel and her people have defied the rules that dictate how much can be accomplished in so short a time. When compared to nations that have existed for centuries, 70 years is "young." And typically, 70 years is not enough time to make large and lasting changes in the world. Yet, we have witnessed the greatest re-birth in human history.

For 2,000 years, the prophecies of the Bible were mostly silent. Yet, during the last 70 years, we have seen the words of the prophets uttered thousands of years ago come to life. Just over 70 years ago, my maternal grandfather was flee-ing for his life from the Nazis in Germany. To-day, my children are growing up in a proud and strong Jewish State.

Seventy years ago, Israel was not a *"land flowing with milk and honey"* (Exodus 3:8), but a patchwork of swampland and desert. Today, the desert blooms — just as Isaiah had prophesied (Isaiah 35:1-2). Seventy years ago, the future of the Jewish people seemed uncertain, with more than a third of the world's Jewish population decimated by the Nazi killing machine. Today we have ris-en from the ashes of the Holocaust and look forward to a bright future as a free people in our own land.

Israel has been reborn.

I can relate to the rebirth of the Jewish people on a personal level. After seven gen-erations of my father's family living in the Holy Land, my great-grandfather was the first to relocate and live in America. My father, Rabbi Yechiel Eckstein, was the first to be born in the United States. By the time I was born, our family was like any other Ameri-can family. With the freedom, opportunities, and standard of living that America offers, it appeared unlikely that my family would ever leave and return to Israel.

Jerusalem today

Yet, by the grace of God, we did return to the Holy Land. First, my father came in 2001; I made *aliyah* (immigrating to Israel) more than a dozen years ago. After I got married, my new husband and I planned to start our lives together in New Jersey. We never did. While we were planning our future, God spoke to my heart and to my husband's heart. We felt that God was calling us home. A week later, we were on a plane to Israel, and we haven't looked back. I am so grateful that my four children were born here in the Holy Land; our family is where it is meant to be once again.

Since then, my grandparents made *aliyah* in 2011, and soon, my older sister, Talia, will be joining us. Four generations of Ecksteins are now united once again in the Jewish homeland. When we open up to God, He opens doors that allow us to do things and go places that we never thought possible.

I see the hand of God in the work of *The Fellowship* as well. Thirty-five years ago, my father had a radical vision that no one

Rabbi Eckstein's parents make aliyah (Yossi Zamir)

thought was possible to achieve — to build bridges of understanding between Jews and Christians based upon shared values and a love of God. To that end, he established *The Fellowship* in 1983. Since then, *The Fellowship* has become the largest non-profit organization in Israel, helping 1.3 million people each year and giving a voice to Christians around the world who stand with the Jewish people.

Growing up, I didn't really understand what my father was accomplishing at *The Fellowship*. When he came home in the evenings, he just wanted to be *Abba* (father) to my two sisters and me. He also wanted to spare us the heartache of knowing that many were attacking him because they disagreed with his work reaching out to the Christian community.

It wasn't until I made *aliyah* and saw for myself *The Fellowship* logo everywhere in Israel that I began to understand the scope of my father's work. I saw *The Fellowship* name on soup kitchens, bomb shelters, and food boxes sent to the elderly. At the same time, I began to meet Christians who were visiting Israel, and I was floored by their unwavering support and love for the Jewish people and the Jewish state.

I discovered that I was extremely passionate about the work of *The Fellowship* — both in providing humanitarian aid and in creating bridges of understanding between Christians

Recipient of Fellowship support thanks Yael Eckstein (IFCJ)

and Jews. My heart was set — I wanted to be a part of my father's groundbreaking and meaningful work.

I had the privilege of joining *The Fellowship* in 2005, and have since gained a great appreciation and understanding both for the people we help on a daily basis and for our steadfast Christian friends who share my love of Israel and her people.

I have learned so much working alongside

X

my father. Now, I'm preparing myself for an even greater role in helping this organization move forward into the next generation as its next president when my father retires. As we celebrate 35 years of *The Fellowship*, I am humbled and honored to be a part of this blessed ministry.

I look forward to seeing what the next 35 years have in store for *The Fellowship* and what the next 70 years will bring for my family, for Israel, and for the entire world. With God's blessings and our Christian friends, the possibilities are limitless!

Yael with little girl Mevaseret Zion
Credit Debbi Cooper(IFCJ)

With blessings from Israel,

Yael Eckstein

Yael Eckstein,
Global Executive Vice President,
September 7, 2018

INTRODUCTION

"'The days are coming,' declares the Lord, 'when I will bring my people Israel and Judah back from captivity and restore them to the land I gave their ancestors to possess,' says the Lord."
— JEREMIAH 30:3

O n Friday, May 14, 1948, two hours before the Sabbath, the state of Israel was declared an independent nation by David Ben-Gurion, Israel's first Prime Minister. He began the declaration with the following words:

> "*Eretz Yisrael* — The Land of Israel — was the birthplace of the Jewish people. Here their spiritual, religious, and political identity was shaped. Here they first attained statehood, created cultural values of national and universal significance and gave to the world the eternal Bible. After being forcibly exiled from their land, the people kept their faith throughout their Dispersion and never ceased to pray and hope for their return to the land and for the restoration in it of their political freedom..."

David Ben-Gurion publicly pronouncing the Declaration of the State of Israel, May 14 1948, Tel Aviv, Israel

After formally declaring the new state of Israel and outlining its intentions for peace and

1

prosperity for all, Ben-Gurion concluded by saying that the document was signed with full trust in the "Rock of Israel."

FOR WHO IS GOD BESIDES THE LORD? AND WHO IS THE ROCK EXCEPT OUR GOD?

— PSALM 18:31

Map of Israel War of Independence, 1948

This was the most dramatic and critical moment in Jewish history since the Jews were exiled from their homeland nearly two millennia earlier. The nation of Israel was reborn, recalling the words of the prophet Isaiah: *"Who has ever heard of such things? Who has ever seen things like this? Can a country be born in a day or a nation be brought forth in a moment? Yet no sooner is Zion in labor than she gives birth to her children"* (Isaiah 66:8).

However, the rebirth of the nation did not come without birthing pains. The very next day after declaring its independence, Israel was attacked by a coalition of Arab armies from Lebanon, Syria, Iraq, Egypt, Saudi Arabia, and Transjordan, and was forced to defend herself in what would be a long, bloody War of Independence. The war gradually ended in 1949 with one percent of its fledgling population having lost their lives.

The Jewish state also lost Jerusalem, which

became occupied by Transjordan, now known as Jordan today. Under Jordanian control, the Jews were forbidden from entering the Jewish Quarter of the Old City of Jerusalem, and more importantly, from praying at the Western Wall, the last remaining vestige of the Holy Temple and one of the most sacred sites in all Judaism. It was a high price to pay, but the state of Israel survived its first major challenge.

War flared again in 1956, when Egyptian leader General Gamal Abdel Nasser nationalized the Suez Canal, an important shipping waterway. Israel, along with British and French forces, fought the Egyptians to regain shipping rights to the canal. The Soviets, in coming to the aid of Egypt, threatened nuclear war in Europe, which led to the U.S. pressuring Britain, France, and Israel to withdraw.

In 1967, Syria, Egypt, and Jordan built up troops along Israel's border. In what became known as the Six-Day War, Israel pre-emptively struck Egypt and miraculously destroyed the Egyptian air force while it was still on the

The Six-Day War, 1967, Jerusalem

ground. In the next days of the war, the Israel Defense Forces (IDF) defended against an attack from Jordan, and in the process, reunified Jerusalem. Jews worldwide shed tears of joy as Jerusalem was once again the unified capital of the Jewish people.

In 1973, Israel was once again thrust into war when the Egyptians and Syrians launched a simultaneous surprise attack on the holiest day on the Jewish calendar, *Yom Kippur*. Initially, the war did not go well for Israel. Heavy casualties were sustained. But ultimately, after three weeks of fighting, Israel gained the upper hand, and with God's help, pushed both

Egyptian military trucks cross a bridge, October 7, 1973

the Egyptian and Syrian armies back, handing them a sound defeat.

After each war, Israel either withdrew or offered to withdraw in exchange for peace and recognition of the Jewish state. Repeatedly, Israel has demonstrated her deep desire to live in peace with the Arab world. In 1979, Israel signed a peace treaty with Egypt, and in 1994, with Jordan.

In addition to four full-scale wars, there have been numerous other acts of aggression against Israel and her people. Since 1948, Israel has been forced to defend herself from a constant threat of terrorism. Thousands of innocent Israelis have been murdered over the last 70 years resulting from these acts of terror.

Yet, despite these challenges, Israel has managed to grow, develop, and become a blessing to the entire world. Israel is known as the "Start-Up Nation" because of the amazing innovations coming from within her borders. Instant messaging, the Pentium chip, Waze (the world's largest traffic and navigation app), and Mobileye (developers of vision-based advanced driver-assistance systems) are just a few examples of the global impact that Israel has made in technology, leading many world financiers to invest in Israel. Within the next few years, Israel, the country that began with nothing, anticipates being one of the world's strongest economies.

> "No country in the history of the world has ever contributed more to humankind and accomplished more for its people in so brief a period of time as Israel has done since its relatively recent rebirth in 1948."
>
> — Alan Dershowitz, American lawyer and scholar

Additionally, Israel is on the forefront of medical breakthroughs as well, producing many lifesaving products and leading research on curing disease. Among its many contributions in the health industry, Israel has produced the PillCam™, a camera so tiny it can be swallowed in order to provide internal imaging of a person's body, and the Emergency Bandage, nicknamed the Israeli bandage, which stops hemorrhaging and applies appropriate pressure to wounds. It was first used for saving lives during NATO peacekeeping operations in Bosnia and Herzegovina.

In the agricultural realm, Israel has gifted the world with the drip irrigation system, which consistently provides small amounts of water to crops, allowing growth in areas otherwise too arid for produce. Israel is pioneering ways to create clean energy and clean water in countries that don't have enough water to live healthy lives. Not to mention that Israel also invented the cherry tomato!

As the Scriptures remind us, *"The desert and the parched land will be glad; the wilderness will rejoice and blossom. Like the crocus, it will burst into bloom; it will rejoice greatly and shout for joy"* (Isaiah 35:1-2a). Israel has not only made their own desert bloom but has brought new life into countries in need around the world.

Finally, Israel is consistently among the first responders whenever there is a natural disaster around the world or when other nations desperately need aid. Israel has helped in the aftermath of tsunamis, earthquakes, and hurricanes. Israelis are among the first to treat Syrian refugees, and Israel treats the wounded of enemy countries in her own hospitals.

As I write this book as a tribute to Israel's triumphs and progress over the past 70 years, it is also important to appreciate the context of this tiny miraculous nation. While modern Israel, by all standards, is very young for a nation, according to the Jewish sages, the very roots of this land can be traced back to Creation!

In order to appreciate the historical and spiritual underpinnings of this Holy Land, I have compiled 70 devotional reflections to help you understand God's covenantal relationship with His land and His chosen people, the Jews. The first ten devotions offer an introduction to God's Holy Land and its people; the ensuing devotions use the acrostic I.S.R.A.E.L. to teach six important truths about God's special bond with Israel and the Jewish people:

I — Important to God
(Genesis 12:3)

S — State of Israel
(Leviticus 20:24)

R — Righteous Giving
(Deuteronomy 15:11)

A — *Aliyah* (immigration to Israel,
Deuteronomy 30:4)

E — Educate yourself and others
about Israel (Psalm 25:5)

L — Love your neighbor
(Leviticus 19:18)

The more we understand and know about Israel, the more we can appreciate God's hand in world events. The more we appreciate the

Jerusalem Day, Credit Ziv Koren

miracle of Israel, the more we can praise God for the great wonders He has done and continues to do in our times. The more we know about one another, the more we can break down thousands of years of animosity and build bridges of understanding.

With prayers for *shalom*, peace

Rabbi Eckstein

Rabbi Yechiel Eckstein,
Founder and President

Jewish immigration to Israel, July 18, 1947

ISRAEL: GOD'S HOLY LAND

*The LORD said to Abram after Lot had parted from him, "Look around
from where you are, to the north and south, to the east and west.
All the land that you see I will give to you and your offspring."*
— GENESIS 13:14–15

God's promise to Abraham created an unbreakable bond between
the Jewish people and the land of Israel. The fulfillment of God's
promises came in the miracle of the Jewish return to their land after
nearly two millennia of dispersion. Never during the long intervening
centuries did the Jews waver in their passionate yearning to return home
to the land God had given them. Never did our love for Israel wane.

Our celebration of Israel expresses more than the joy of a fledgling
nation that beat the odds and serves as a beacon of light to the world. It
is the celebration of God's word coming to fruition, the Bible coming
full circle, and our world entering a new phase for all humanity, when
all prophecies regarding this wondrous time and land will be fulfilled.

*God's Promise to Abraham by
Julius Schnorr von Carolsfeld,
Woodcut for "Die Bibel in
Bildern", 1860*

Israel: Devotion 1

"THE LORD IS MY ROCK"

THE LORD IS MY ROCK,
MY FORTRESS AND MY
DELIVERER; MY GOD IS
MY ROCK, IN WHOM
I TAKE REFUGE, MY
SHIELD AND THE HORN
OF MY SALVATION, MY
STRONGHOLD.
— Psalm 18:2

Just before the modern state of Israel declared her independence, there was a fierce debate. The religious Jews insisted that the name of God be included in the official Declaration of Independence document. But the secular, non-religious sector wanted religion out of it. It was Friday, May 14, 1948, and all parties wanted to be officially independent before the start of the Sabbath. They reached a compromise. Instead of using one of the traditional names of God, He would be referred to as "the Rock of Israel." This was vague enough for the non-religious, yet significant enough for the believers.

In Psalm 18, David refers to God as his rock. What does this poetic, yet ambiguous term mean? As David specified in his psalm, a rock was a shield, a horn, a stronghold.

A rock can be used as a shield. Held in front of you, a rock can deflect all kinds of harmful objects. David recognized that God was his shield and protector when he went into battle. Remember his very first fight against the Philistine giant, Goliath? King Saul offered his armor to David to wear into battle, but David refused. Instead, he chose to go into battle armed with the name of God.

A rock can also be a weapon. In the Scriptures, a horn is a symbol of power and might. Animals use their horns to attack. Without it, they would be powerless. David recognized that God was his greatest weapon. In Psalm 18, David acknowledged that his military victories had very little to do with him and *everything* to do with the Lord. Without God, he would have been crushed by King Saul long before he ever ascended the throne.

Finally, a rock, in the form of a cave, can be a stronghold. When David was hiding from King Saul, he took refuge in a deserted cave. Saul's men were not far behind, and they, too, found the same cave. But they didn't enter it. Why? According to Jewish tradition, God had a spider spin a web in the moments after David had entered it. When Saul's men saw the web, they assumed no one could have possibly entered the cave and so left. The physical rock cave may have provided a safe refuge, but God provided David's protection.

When we call God our rock, we recognize that He is our savior and protector. We recognize that without Him, we are vulnerable and exposed. How fortuitous that this became the term used in Israel's Declaration of Independence. They couldn't have picked a better one!

At the outset of the modern Israeli state, it was made clear that Israel would be independent from everyone. That is, except for God. God was, is, and always will be the Rock of Israel. God is Israel's foundation, without whom, she could not stand.

Designate God as your rock. Remember that He is not far away in the distance. God is with you, protecting you and fighting your battles. Even in turbulent times, He will be your solid ground.

Israel: Devotion 2

OUR SOURCE OF STRENGTH

The Six-Day War — Israeli tanks advancing on the Golan Heights, June 10, 1967

ALL YOU ISRAELITES, TRUST IN THE LORD — HE IS THEIR HELP AND SHIELD.
— Psalm 115:9

The Israel Defense Forces (IDF) is one of the greatest armies in the world. From daring rescue missions to winning ground battles against all odds, the IDF has surprised the world time and time again. But what is the source of Israel's strength? Israel herself is still finding out.

Two of Israel's greatest battles came in relatively quick succession of each other, but each played out very differently. In 1967, Israel fought the Six-Day War. In response to a threat from the Arab world, Israel's military reacted swiftly and strongly. The whole war was won in less than a week!

Jews and Israel supporters everywhere felt both awe and pride. Perhaps a little too much pride. Israel's slogan after the Six-Day War was "All the honor to the Israel Defense Forces." Certainly, the IDF deserved credit. But not enough credit was given to God. Scripture tells us, *"For the LORD your God is the one who goes with you to fight for you against your enemies to give you victory"* (Deuteronomy 20:4). All of Israel's battles are fought and won by Him.

Israeli tank on the Golan Heights, October 1, 1973

The *Yom Kippur War*, fought in 1973, was a completely different experience for Israel. The war was unexpected; the army, unprepared. Syria attacked and outnumbered Israel. One particularly memorable battle was fought in a place now known as "The Valley of Tears," due to the loss of life during the fierce combat that took place there.

The attack happened at night, and the Syrians had over 1,000 tanks, equipped with night-vision technology. Israel had less than 200 tanks, none of which had night-vision capability. Israel was outnumbered and unequipped. But guess who won? God performed great miracles, and while Israel sustained heavy casualties, she defeated her enemies.

Battles such as this one are the reason why Israel's motto changed after the *Yom Kippur* War. It became "Israel trusts in God," based on Psalm 115:9: *"All you Israelites, trust in the* LORD — *He is their help and shield."* Everyone realized that God was behind the miracle. It was no accident that the war began on *Yom Kippur*, the holiest day of the year. Almost every Jew had spent that day engaged in prayer and fasting. Those are the "weapons" that helped win the war.

More than 3,000 years ago, a tiny David went out to fight a massive Goliath. He said: *"You come against me with sword and spear and javelin, but I come to you in the name of the* LORD *Almighty..."* (1 Samuel 17:45). Then David went on to slay the mighty giant against all odds.

So it was and so it always will be: Israel's source of strength and protection — and ours — is God.

Israel: Devotion 3

WE CAN DO ANYTHING THROUGH GOD

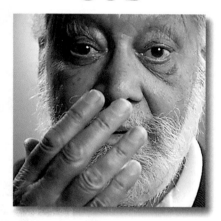

BUT MOSES SAID
TO THE LORD,
"SINCE I SPEAK WITH
FALTERING LIPS, WHY
WOULD PHARAOH
LISTEN TO ME?"

— Exodus 6:30

Have you ever wondered why when God needed a leader unlike any that the world had ever seen, He turned to the verbally challenged Moses? We might have thought that God would have called on someone like a Martin Luther King Jr., who could turn out a passionate speech like *"I Have a Dream."* Or God could have picked a leader like a witty Winston Churchill or a charismatic John F. Kennedy. But God turned instead to the humble and meek Moses, who said, *"Since I speak with faltering lips, why would Pharaoh listen to me?"* (Exodus 6:30)

Basically, Moses was saying, "I am totally unfit for this job! I lack the talent and ability to fulfill the mission! Why God would you pick me?" And yet, as so often happens, that is exactly how God works.

Think about it. God chose David, a young shepherd boy who was too small to even wear King Saul's armor, to slaughter the giant Goliath. God chose Joseph, the most hated of his brothers, a slave, and then a prison inmate, to become the Prime Minister of Egypt and provide for his entire family. God chose Jael, a young woman, to slaughter the mighty warrior Sisera when the entire army of Israel had failed to do so. He chose Esther, an orphaned Jewish girl in exile, to become the Queen of Persia and save her people, Israel.

God often chooses individuals who seem the most unlikely candidates to fill the most important roles. He does this because He wants us to know that it's not our

Moses views the Promised Land *by Julius Schnorr von Carolsfeld, 1860*

talents and abilities that determine the outcomes, but His will and His miracles that bring about salvation. As we read in Zechariah 4:6, *"'Not by might nor by power, but by my Spirit,' says the* LORD *Almighty."*

In 1948, when the United Nations voted to reinstate the state of Israel, the fledgling country, made up at the time mostly of refugees and Holocaust survivors, was attacked by a coalition of Arab armies. Yet, Israel was victorious. Israel, the modern-day David, slew the modern-day Goliaths. Israel accomplished what no one expected. Everyone predicted a slaughter. In fact, they were already digging the graves of the new Israelis. But God's will prevailed, Israel prevailed, and Israel will continue to prevail because of God's will.

I want to encourage us all today not to be intimidated by a task that seems too large. When God calls us to do something, don't look at what you lack. Don't be scared off by what you "can't" do. Through God, we can do anything and be anything. God chooses the willing, not necessarily the able.

He has chosen and promoted many imperfect people in past — and He can choose us, too.

Israel: Devotion 4

SOWING SEEDS

THOSE WHO GO OUT
WEEPING, CARRYING
SEED TO SOW, WILL
RETURN WITH SONGS
OF JOY, CARRYING
SHEAVES WITH THEM.

— Psalm 126:6

During the *Yom Kippur* War in 1973, a soldier asked this moving question to then Prime Minister Golda Meir: "My father was killed in the War (of Independence in) 1948, and we won. My uncle was killed in the war of '56, and we won. My brother lost an arm in the '67 war, and we won. Last week, I lost my best friend over there … and we're going to win. But is all of our sacrifice worthwhile, Golda?"

In Psalm 126, the psalmist writes: *"Those who go out weeping, carrying seed to sow, will return with songs of joy, carrying sheaves with them."* This verse is often quoted in reference to the rebirth of the state of Israel, and it can be found on many buildings and monuments across the land.

Israelis have spent much time weeping as they sowed the seeds of a new country. Some of those sacrifices have come in the form of working long days in the hot sun; others have come in the form of the ultimate sacrifice — losing a loved one or one's own life.

True, we have seen much fruit. Today Israel is a beautiful country with a thriving economy. However, we have not achieved our ultimate goal of being a safe people in our own land. Israelis still suffer from terror, war, and the loss of life. Is it worth it?

Here is how Golda Meir answered the soldier on that day in 1973: "I weep for your loss, just as I grieve for all our dead. I lie awake at night thinking of them. And, I must tell you in all honesty, were our sacrifices for ourselves alone, then perhaps you would be right; I'm not at all sure they would be worthwhile. But if our sacrifices are for the sake of the whole Jewish people, then I believe with all my heart that any price is worthwhile."

Golda Meir, Israeli PM, March 1, 1973

Sometimes individuals or nations have to make difficult decisions for the sake of future generations. But remember, the freedom and prosperity that we enjoy today came from the blood, tears, and yes, sometimes the lives, of those who came before us. We owe it to them to do what they did for us, for our own children. Though we may weep as we plant, there will be joy in the future.

An ancient Jewish story speaks about a *Torah* scholar named Honi who once saw a man planting a carob tree. "Don't you know that a carob tree takes 70 years to bear fruit? You won't see the fruit in your lifetime!" The man answered Honi, "My fathers planted before me, and today I enjoy their fruit. I plant for my children."

What seeds will you sow today?

Israel: Devotion 5

HOPE AND FAITH FOR THE FUTURE

"BLESSED ARE YOU, ISRAEL! WHO IS LIKE YOU, A PEOPLE SAVED BY THE LORD? HE IS YOUR SHIELD AND HELPER AND YOUR GLORIOUS SWORD. YOUR ENEMIES WILL COWER BEFORE YOU, AND YOU WILL TREAD ON THEIR HEIGHTS."

— Deuteronomy 33:29

When former Israeli National Security Advisor Yossi Cohen was named head of the *Mossad*, Israel's intelligence agency, he noted that Israel was only established because of the help of God and that God's help is just as needed today. And Cohen was right! It has often been said that Israel's secret weapon is faith. More accurately, Israel's greatest weapon is God, yet it is our faith in Him that activates His intervention.

In Deuteronomy, after Moses had concluded blessing each of the twelve tribes of Israel, just prior to his death, Moses gave a general blessing to the entire nation. He said: *"Blessed are you, Israel! Who is like you, a people saved by the LORD? He is your shield and helper and your glorious sword. Your enemies will cower before you, and you will tread on their heights"* (Deuteronomy 33:29).

The Jewish sages explain that it is precisely because Israel looks to God as our *"shield and helper"* that God becomes our *"glorious sword,"* allowing us to overcome our enemies. Indeed, our faith is what has helped Israel overcome overwhelming odds and the reason why we are still here.

Kaiser Wilhelm I in 1884

In the 1800s, the Kaiser of Prussia asked his head advisor if he could prove the existence of God. Otto Von Bismarck replied, "The Jews, Sir, the Jews." There is no natural explanation for how a tiny group of people, twice exiled from their land, and persecuted repeatedly for millennium, could still be around today.

Moreover, the fact that the Jewish people have returned to their homeland, a feat never accomplished by any other nation, is nothing less than miraculous. As Moses said, *"Who is like you, a people saved by the LORD?"* The only explanation for the miracle of the existence of the Jewish people and the state of Israel, is the existence of God.

However, what I love most about this verse is that it instills hope and inspires faith for the future. Just as God has helped Israel beat the odds for the past 70 years, we can be sure that He will continue to do so for the next 70 years — and longer! Even as Israel faces unprecedented challenges today, we can trust in God for unparalleled salvation.

We are watching history unfold before our very eyes. We are watching ancient prophecies come to fruition. And like Israel, when we activate our faith, we can activate God's intervention during these tumultuous times. The God of Israel is great. The God of Israel lives. And the God of Israel will protect and guide all who call to Him.

As Scriptures say: *"The LORD is near to all who call on him, to all who call on him in truth"* (Psalm 145:18).

Israel: Devotion 6

LIVING PROPHECIES

"THEY WILL PLANT VINEYARDS AND DRINK THEIR WINE; THEY WILL MAKE GARDENS AND EAT THEIR FRUIT. I WILL PLANT ISRAEL IN THEIR OWN LAND, NEVER AGAIN TO BE UPROOTED FROM THE LAND I HAVE GIVEN THEM," SAYS THE LORD YOUR GOD.

— Amos 9:14–15

In 1867, Mark Twain visited the Holy Land. This is what he saw: "A desolate country … given over wholly to weeds … a silent mournful expanse … a desolation … we never saw a human being on the whole route … hardly a tree or shrub anywhere. Even the olive tree and the cactus, those fast friends of a worthless soil, had almost deserted the country." The land that Mark Twain saw was the way that the land looked for more than two thousand years. As foretold in the Bible, once the children of Israel were exiled, the land ceased to blossom.

In Leviticus 19:2, God gave the command to His people to *"Be holy."* This command was followed with a series of do's and don'ts that would lead the people onto this path of holiness. When God gives a command, it is not to be taken lightly. As is evident from this passage from Amos, failure to heed God's Word can lead to disastrous consequences.

The prophet Amos was addressing a wayward nation who had strayed from this path of holiness, and he told the Israelites that they would be exiled from their land. As God had warned His children back in Leviticus, *"'Keep all my decrees and laws and follow them, so that the land where I am bringing you to live may not vomit you out'"* (Leviticus 20:22). Once the children of Israel failed to keep the laws of the Lord, it was only a matter of time before they would be spit out. And indeed, they were.

For 2,000 years, the nation of Israel was exiled from the land of Israel. During that time, it was as if the land itself was in mourning. This is how Mark Twain found the land in 1867. But history was about to advance to the next stage mentioned in the verses from Amos: *"... I will bring my people Israel back from exile. They will rebuild the ruined cities ..."* God promised to return the people of Israel to their land. And indeed, He has.

Reading the rest of the verses from Amos, one can hardly believe that the prophet is talking about the same land that Mark Twain had seen. He describes cities with vineyards, plentiful wine, abundant vegetation and fruit. Yet, this is a perfect description of Israel today. Miraculously, the "silent mournful expanse" has been transformed into an abundant garden!

Mark Twain in 1867

Friends, we are living in these miraculous times and watching biblical prophecies unfold before our very eyes. At *The Fellowship*, our mission is to help Christians and Jews come together in contributing to God's purposes. In the end, God's Word will be fulfilled, but we can choose to play a part in the unfolding of His plan.

Israel: Devotion 7

STRENGTH IN UNITY

"'FIVE OF YOU WILL
CHASE A HUNDRED,
AND A HUNDRED
OF YOU WILL CHASE
TEN THOUSAND, AND
YOUR ENEMIES WILL
FALL BY THE SWORD
BEFORE YOU.'"
— Leviticus 26:8

An old farmer had five sons who couldn't get along. When the aged farmer felt that his time was near, he called his sons to his deathbed and advised them to live in unity. It was clear to him that his sons ignored his advice.

The farmer asked a servant to bring in a bundle of sticks. He asked each son to try and break the bundle, but not one succeeded. Then he ordered the servant to untie the bundle and set the sticks free. Now the sons could easily break all the sticks that had been in the bundle. The father urged his sons to live like the bundle of sticks — together they would be strong and unbreakable; but if they separated from each other, all would be vulnerable to harm.

Earlier in chapter 26 of Leviticus, God had given a series of blessings that would come upon His children of Israel *"if you follow my decrees and are careful to obey my commands"* (Leviticus 26:3). There would be plenty of rain, an abundance of crops, and peace. When it came to the promises about safety and security,

God gave this blessing: *"'Five of you will chase a hundred, and a hundred of you will chase ten thousand...'"* Few would defeat many, and this blessing came true for Israel both in biblical times and in modern times as well.

However, as the Jewish sages point out, the math in this verse doesn't add up. If five can chase 100, then that is a ratio of 1-to-20. If that is the kind of strength that God is promising, then 100 Israelites should be able to defeat 2,000.

Yet the verse promises that 100 men will chase 10,000! That's a ratio of 1-to-100!

The sages clarify this apparent inconsistency by explaining that we cannot compare the unity of five people with the unity of 100. As the old farmer tried to teach his sons, there is strength in unity. The greater the unity, the greater the strength.

United we stand, and united we are blessed. This is why I founded the *International Fellowship of Christians and Jews* in 1983. Together, Christians and Jews, we are millions of people united together for the sake of Israel. Alone, each of us can do some good, but together as partners, we are having a major impact on God's land and His people. Together we can continue to bring great strength and blessings to Israel, and God will bless us in return. As He promises in Genesis: *"I will bless those who bless you"* (12:3).

Israel: Devotion 8

A PRAYER FOR THE WORLD

PRAY FOR THE
PEACE OF JERUSALEM:
"MAY THOSE WHO
LOVE YOU BE SECURE."
— Psalm 122:6

P*ray for the peace of Jerusalem"* is one of the most well-known lines from the Psalms. It has been made into songs; it is said as a prayer by millions around the world. Most of us understand how badly Jerusalem — whose very name comes from the word *shalom*, peace — needs our prayers for the peace that has eluded her for over 3,000 years. However, what many of us don't realize is that when we pray for Jerusalem, we are essentially praying for ourselves.

It has been said that whatever happens in Israel will determine the fate of the world. Israel is a country smaller than the state of New Jersey with a population that is less than 1 percent of humanity, yet Israel continues to make world headlines daily. That's because Israel is at the epicenter of the war between good and evil, peace and terror. So whatever happens in Jerusalem is bound to impact the rest of the world.

Spiritually speaking, this makes perfect

sense. Jewish tradition teaches that when God made the world, creation began in Jerusalem. This is where everything began, and it is also where everything will end. Mount Moriah in Jerusalem is the place that Jacob called *"the house of God ... the gate of heaven"* (Genesis 28:17). Jewish sages describe Jerusalem as the heart of the world — and a body is only as healthy as its heart.

This is why the next words in verse 6 of Psalm 122 are: *"May those who love you be secure."* Those who love Jerusalem and pray for her peace bring peace and security upon themselves. Only when Jerusalem is secure can we hope to find security for ourselves.

Have you prayed for the peace of Jerusalem today? I cannot think of a more important prayer. Pray for Jerusalem today and every day, because if we can heal the heart of the world, the rest of the body will follow. Heal Jerusalem, and we will heal the world.

Height 743 section of Jerusalem map (1925) showing location of Mount Zion according to Jewish sources, also known as Mount Moriah

Israel: Devotion 9
"THE SILVER PLATTER"

Ben-Gurion (left) signing the Declaration of Independence held by Moshe Sharet

REMEMBER THE DAYS
OF OLD; CONSIDER THE
GENERATIONS LONG PAST.
ASK YOUR FATHER AND
HE WILL TELL YOU, YOUR
ELDERS, AND THEY WILL
EXPLAIN TO YOU.

— Deuteronomy 32:7

In Deuteronomy we read, *"Remember the days of old; consider the generations long past. Ask your father and he will tell you, your elders, and they will explain to you."* (Deuteronomy 32:7). Remembering the past has always been a foundational value in Judaism.

In 1947, just after Israel had won the United Nations vote for a Jewish state, David Ben-Gurion, the first prime minister of Israel, said these poignant words: "When I returned to Jerusalem I saw the city happy and rejoicing, dancing in the streets and a big crowd gathering in the yard of the Jewish Agency building. I'll admit the truth —

David Ben-Gurion in 1959

that joy was not my lot — not because I did not appreciate the U.N.'s decision, but because I knew what awaited us: war with all the armies of the Arab nations."

These chilling words were the truth. Before the dream of nationhood could be realized, there would be much war, bloodshed, and tears.

Around that same time, Chaim Weizmann, the first president of Israel, made a similar remark that later became famous. He said, "The state will not be given to the Jewish people on a silver platter." He, too, realized that there would be a dear price to pay for Israel's nation-

Chaim Weizmann in 1949

hood. Picking up on those words, Israeli poet Natan Alterman wrote a beautiful, yet heart-wrenching poem called *"The Silver Platter."*

In it, he depicts a young boy and girl, dirty and exhausted from battle. As they approach, they are asked "Who are you?" They answer, "We are the silver platter on which the Jewish state was given." The poem concludes, "Thus they will say and fall back in shadows. And the rest will be told in the chronicles of Israel."

Every year on *Yom HaZikaron*, Israel's Memorial Day, we remember those young men and women who sacrificed their lives so that we could have a homeland. We honor those who became the "silver platter" on which our state was given to us. We bring them out of the shadows of the past and tell their stories again and again so we don't forget the sacrifices that were made so that Israel can live.

Let us pray that no other lives need be sacrificed to ensure the freedom, the security, and the peace, *shalom*, we all deserve.

Israel: Devotion 10

A NATION REBORN

"WHO HAS EVER HEARD OF SUCH THINGS? WHO HAS EVER SEEN THINGS LIKE THIS? CAN A COUNTRY BE BORN IN A DAY OR A NATION BE BROUGHT FORTH IN A MOMENT? YET NO SOONER IS ZION IN LABOR THAN SHE GIVES BIRTH TO HER CHILDREN."

— Isaiah 66:8

In 1948, at 4 p.m. on the 4th of the Hebrew month of *Lyar*, the British lowered their flag over the land, ending nearly two millennia of foreign occupation. Immediately, Israel raised her own flag. The flag, which was designed in 1897 by the First Zionist Congress, was white, to symbolize newness and purity. It had two blue stripes, the color of heaven, to resemble a prayer shawl, symbolizing the Jewish tradition.

In the center was placed the Star of David, recalling the first King of Israel to rule from the capital of Jerusalem. While the Jews were forcibly pushed out of their land thousands of years earlier, they had never stopped trying to resettle the land or longing to reinstate their sovereignty. At last, the dream had become a reality, seemingly overnight.

Thousands of years earlier, the prophet Isaiah wrote: *"Who has ever heard of such things? Who has ever seen things like this? Can a country be born in a day or a nation be brought forth in a moment?"* Those words could have very well been written on May 14, 1948, when Israel declared herself an independent nation once again. Miraculously, after nearly 2,000 years, the prophecy had been fulfilled, and more biblical prophecies continue to be fulfilled as Israel is resurrected and her children return home.

David Ben-Gurion, Israel's first prime minister, read the Declaration of Independence over the radio on the eve of the Sabbath as many wept for joy. He began, "The land of Israel was the birthplace of the Jewish people. Here the spiritual, religious, and national identity was formed. Here they achieved independence

The Prophet Isaiah *by Julius Schnorr von Carolsfeld, Woodcut for "Die Bibel in Bildern", 1860*

and created a culture of national and universal significance. Here they wrote and gave the Bible to the world…"

Once Ben-Gurion finished reading the declaration, a blessing was made praising God for bringing us to that day, followed by the Israeli National Anthem, *Hatikvah,* "The Hope."

Friends, let us open our eyes and see the miracle of it all. Let us praise God for all that He has done and recommit ourselves to doing our part in bringing about the complete fulfillment of every biblical prophecy and every one of God's promises.

IMPORTANT TO GOD

"I will bless those who bless you, and whoever curses you I will curse;
and all peoples on earth will be blessed through you."
— GENESIS 12:3

Even before Creation, according to Jewish tradition, God took the land of Israel and called it His own. He gave it to His chosen people, sealed in the covenant He made with His servant, Abraham, more than three thousand years ago. Over the centuries, God's love for His land and for His people has never waned. As the Bible tells us, *"It is a land the LORD your God cares for; the eyes of the LORD your God are continually on it from the beginning of the year to its end"* (Deuteronomy 11:12).

From God's promises to Abraham came a family, then a tribe, then a nation. It is through this nation, Israel, and these people, the Jews, that the world has been blessed. In the Christian Bible, the Apostle Paul taught that Christians have been grafted onto this rich olive tree that is Israel. The Jewish-educated Paul wrote, *"And you Gentiles, who were branches from a wild olive tree, have been grafted in. So now you also receive the blessing God has promised Abraham and his children, sharing in the rich nourishment from the root of God's special olive tree."* (Romans 11:17, NLT).

Israel is important because it is an eternal reminder of God's love for us.

Important to God: Devotion 1

FROM THE BEGINNING

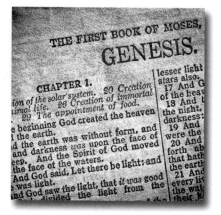

IN THE BEGINNING
GOD CREATED
THE HEAVENS AND
THE EARTH.

— Genesis 1:1

In the beginning" is a fitting title for the story about the creation of the world. They also are the words that begin the entire Bible. The Jewish sages, however, were bothered by this and they asked, "Why? Why not? It seems to make perfect sense to begin any book at *"the beginning."* Would it make more sense to start in the middle or at the end?

The answer depends on what kind of book you are writing. A history book should start at the beginning of history. A storybook should start at the beginning of the story. But the sages understood that the Bible is neither. It was not given to teach us history or to entertain us with a nice story. The *Torah* is an instruction manual for living. Anything it contains is there to teach us about God and how to live our lives.

Since that's the case, the sages felt that it would have been more appropriate to start with the first commandment given to man or a story with a moral. But instead, the *Torah* begins with a description of Creation. The sages ask,

"What does this have to do with the way that we should live?"

Open your heart and hear the answer. It was given thousands of years ago, but couldn't be more relevant today.

The sages taught that one day, the nations of the world were going to come to the Jewish people and say, "You are robbers! You stole the land that you live on!" And they would try to take the land away from the Jews and give it to someone else.

Is this not an accurate description of what is happening in the land of Israel today? Many in the world are working very hard to take Jerusalem from the Jews and the Jews from Judea.

The sages explain that God begins the Bible with Creation so that we would know that *He* created the world and has all authority over the universe. The land on this earth is His to give and His to take away. Only He has the right to do so. He states very clearly in the Bible that He gave the land of Israel, a small portion of the entire earth, to the children of Israel. No one, not even the United Nations, has the right to take that land away.

God begins the Bible with a message for the critical moments at the end of time. He wants us to be strong and unwavering in our support

Creation Day 4
by Julius Schnorr von Carolsfeld, 1860

of Israel. No matter what the world may say, the only voice that matters to us is the Word of God. It is the very first message from God and should be our top priority, too!

Important to God: Devotion 2

UNLOCKING GOD'S BLESSINGS

"I WILL BLESS THOSE WHO BLESS YOU, AND WHOEVER CURSES YOU I WILL CURSE; AND ALL PEOPLES ON EARTH WILL BE BLESSED THROUGH YOU."

— Genesis 12:3

God's gifts come in all shapes and sizes. Sometimes they come in the form of an unexpected check, and other times in the form of healing. Everyone wants to be showered with God's many blessings, but not everyone knows how. What's the key that unlocks the gates of God's favor?

Genesis 12 gives us the answer. God said to Abraham: *"I will bless those who bless you…and all peoples on earth will be blessed through you."* God makes the answer very clear. Those who bless the Jewish people will be rewarded with many blessings themselves.

Here at *The Fellowship*, we have seen how God makes good on His promise. We have received countless letters from people who choose to give to God's people and then find themselves inexplicably blessed as well. Here is just one example of the many stories that we receive:

Jay and Jo Anne are a benevolent couple who enjoy giving wisely. After hearing about

The Fellowship, they decided on an amount of money that they wished to contribute — enough for one Jew to return home for every member of their family. Then, unexpectedly, Jay and Jo Anne received four checks in the same day. But the most amazing part was that when they added all of the money up, it was exactly the amount that they had planned to donate!

Jay said, "It became pretty clear that God wanted us to give to the Jewish people." And that was just the beginning of the "bless fest" that God orchestrated between needy, hurting Jews and Jay and Jo Anne. This couple gave to all aspects of *The Fellowship*'s ministry — from food boxes, to orphanages, to bringing Jews back to Israel. Jay shares what happened next.

"A floodgate of blessings opened up for our family in a very short period of time. Our adult children received pay raises, our granddaughter who had severe food allergies was healed, and many other spiritual and emotional healings took place throughout our immediate and extended family."

It is our hope at *The Fellowship* that you will be inspired by Jay and Jo Anne's story. As Scripture reminds us, *"He who is the Glory of Israel does not lie or change his mind"* (1 Samuel 15:29). God does not go back on His word. What God says in Genesis 12 is true forever! Those who bless the Jewish people and the state of Israel will undoubtedly enjoy great blessings themselves.

Important to God: Devotion 3

LIKE THE STARS

HE TOOK HIM
OUTSIDE AND SAID,
"LOOK UP AT THE SKY
AND COUNT THE STARS
— IF INDEED YOU CAN
COUNT THEM." THEN HE
SAID TO HIM, "SO SHALL
YOUR OFFSPRING BE."

— Genesis 15:5

God's Promise to Abraham
*by Julius Schnorr von
Carolsfeld, 1860*

When Abraham first began his journey, God promised him that he would become a great nation. But now in their 70s and 80s, Abraham and Sarah begin to wonder if that nation will be born from children of their own. Abraham decided, *"You have given me no children; so a servant in my household will be my heir"* (Genesis 15:3). Abraham concluded that the nation will be built by his close disciple, Eliezer. Perhaps the aging couple would remain childless after all.

Not so, said God. He reassured Abraham that he will have children and that his descendants will be many. How many? God told Abraham, *"Look up at the sky and count the stars."* Can anyone, even with the most sophisticated technology, count all of the stars? *"So shall your offspring be,"* said God.

Was God just teaching Abraham about the quantity of his offspring, or was he teaching him something about their quality as well? According to the Jewish sages, the stars are an analogy not just for the number of Abraham's descendants, but also for their nature as well.

How does a star appear in the night sky? Tiny. A mere speck of light in the vast sky. But what's the reality? Every star is like the sun. Every tiny speck of light in the sky is really a brilliant orbit of light. If we were to get close enough, we would be blinded by their brilliance.

And that's how we need to see the descendants of Abraham. Those who follow God may not always appear to be bright and shiny. Sometimes they might even appear rather dull and tiny. But the truth is that they are huge and brilliant up in the heavens. Some of the brightest stars in heaven look small and lowly here on Earth.

When you look at another person, especially a child, remember that he or she is like a star. He might seem small to you. It might look like she hasn't accomplished much, or that he might not amount to anything great. But what do you really know? Can you know who shines brightly up above? Can you know who is a superstar in God's eyes?

Try to see every person as a hidden luminary, with unknowable potential to illuminate the world. When we see people for the bright and shiny stars that they are, they may just learn to see themselves that way, too.

Important to God: Devotion 4

TAKING IT TO THE STREETS

The Caravan of Abraham *by James Tissot, watercolor, circa 1896–1902, The Jewish Museum, New York*

"I WILL ESTABLISH MY COVENANT AS AN EVERLASTING COVENANT BETWEEN ME AND YOU AND YOUR DESCENDANTS AFTER YOU FOR THE GENERATIONS TO COME, TO BE YOUR GOD AND THE GOD OF YOUR DESCENDANTS AFTER YOU."

— Genesis 17:7

As we read in Chapter 17 of Genesis, God had chosen Abram, or Abraham as he was now called, for a unique mission that would greatly shape the world. God created a covenant between Himself and Abraham and all of Abraham's descendants until the end of time.

The Jewish sages ask: Why Abraham? Why was Abraham chosen for this lofty position? Indeed, as the sages point out, Abraham was not the first to discover the one, true God. In fact, Noah's son and grandson — Shem and Eber — were fully aware of God and even opened up an academy for the study of monotheism and ethics. Why weren't they, who preceded Abraham, chosen instead?

The sages explain that Shem and Eber only taught a few select individuals who would approach them and ask to be taught. Abraham, in contrast, took his teachings to the streets. Literally. Abraham pitched his tent near a busy ancient intersection and set up an inn. There he would offer free food, drinks, a place to sleep, and words about life and God.

It was Abraham's concern for other people and his desire to share the truth with them that made him the perfect man for God's great mission. Only a person who cared deeply for those around him would be suitable as a messenger of God.

The following story illustrates this point even further. According to Jewish tradition, Elijah the prophet miraculously appeared to a certain rabbi shortly after the destruction of the Temple in Jerusalem. The rabbi had gone to the holy site in order to pray. Elijah asked, "My son, why did you go into this ruin?" The rabbi answered, "To pray." Elijah scolded him and said, "You should have prayed on the road."

What is the meaning of this story and why would Elijah consider prayers on the road as more powerful than praying at the holiest place on earth? The sages explain that Elijah

was teaching the rabbi that while it was noble to pray on the holy Temple grounds, it is more important to bring holiness to all grounds.

Abraham's life was all about kindness. He brought ideas of morality, ethics, and godliness into real life where people could encounter them firsthand. Like Abraham, we must also reach out to others with kindness and compassion. While prayer and study are important and praiseworthy, we need to take the ideals that we learn in our churches and synagogues and take them "into the streets." We must feed the hungry and

The True Fast —
Giving Bread to the Hungry,
Isaiah 58

clothe the poor, help a stranger, and be compassionate to our own family members.

In this way, we will be God's partners in spreading His light and perfecting the world.

Important to God: Devotion 5

A TIME FOR JUDGMENT

Jeremiah Lamenting the Destruction of Jerusalem
by Rembrandt, oil on oak panel, 1630, Rijksmuseum

"THEY WILL CHOP DOWN HER FOREST," DECLARES THE LORD, "DENSE THOUGH IT BE. THEY ARE MORE NUMEROUS THAN LOCUSTS, THEY CANNOT BE COUNTED."

— Jeremiah 46:23

In these verses from the prophet Jeremiah, we read about the pending destruction of Egypt, words of destruction eerily similar to those Moses spoke hundreds of years earlier to a different Egyptian pharaoh. The times had changed but the story remained the same. Would Egypt ever learn?

In describing the destruction that would come to Egypt, God said, *"They will chop down her forest," declares the* LORD, *"dense though it be. They are more numerous than locusts ..."* In describing the enemies about to conquer Egypt, God compared them to locusts. This wasn't by accident. This is a direct reference to one of the 10 plagues that struck Egypt in Moses' time. By making this connection, God was telling Egypt that they should have learned from their past. But they didn't.

After the monumental and miraculous destruction of Egypt brought about in Moses' time, you would think that Egypt had learned its lesson and would never touch Israel again. Yet, we read in 1 Kings 14:25–26 that just after King Solomon's death, Shishak, king of Egypt, ransacked Jerusalem and even audaciously stole all Solomon's gold shields. Later, in 2 Kings 23:29–30, the Egyptian Pharaoh Necho killed the righteous king of Judah, Josiah. Numerous times throughout biblical history Egypt violated Israel's trust and either attacked or betrayed her.

Through His prophet Jeremiah, God was saying enough is enough. The time for judgment had come.

Today, we have to ask the same question: Will Israel's enemies ever learn? Throughout history, God has punished those who oppress Israel. Why do nations continue to provoke Him?

In the second part of Genesis 12:3, God says, *"whoever curses you I will curse."* As God said, it will be. Take a look at Joel 3:1–2, *"In those days and at that time, when I restore the fortunes of Judah and Jerusalem, I will gather all nations and bring them down to the Valley of Jehoshaphat. There I will put them on trial for what they did to my inheritance, my people Israel, because they scattered my people among the nations and divided up my land."*

God has restored the Jewish people to Judah. The nations have already divided up the land. Only a time for judgment remains. As two parts of the prophecy have already come true, we must have faith that the rest will be fulfilled in due time. Those who oppose Israel would be wise to take heed.

However, Genesis 12:3 also teaches us that, *"I will bless those who bless you."* God will bless those who bless Israel. Now, perhaps more than ever, Israel and God's people need friends. Take a stand. Speak up for Israel. Pray for Israel. Bless Israel today, and may God bless you in return.

Important to God: Devotion 6

A GOOD CHALLENGE

Galilee landscape

YOU GRUMBLED IN
YOUR TENTS AND SAID,
"THE LORD HATES US; SO
HE BROUGHT US OUT OF
EGYPT TO DELIVER US
INTO THE HANDS OF THE
AMORITES TO DESTROY US."

— Deuteronomy 1:27

A colleague once shared a statement that profoundly changed the way he viewed his life. This friend is a rabbi in one of the most isolated Jewish communities in the world. One day, a Jewish musician came to town, and after the concert, my friend and the musician began talking. My friend told the musician how hard it was to be a rabbi in such a remote and small Jewish community. "It's extremely difficult," he said with a sigh. The holy musician replied, "Who says easier is better?"

In today's Scripture, Moses was recalling a time when the Israelites were sure that easier was better. They complained to Moses that God had brought them out of Egypt, a lush and bountiful land, in order to go to Israel, an arid part of the world and a place heavily guarded by its inhabitants. As they put it, *"The LORD hates us; so he brought us out of Egypt ..."*

The Jewish sages explain what the Israelites meant with a parable: Imagine a king who has two sons and two fields, one field well irrigated and one dry and parched. To the son he loves, he gave the irrigated field; to the one he hates, he gave the arid field. The land of Egypt is irrigated, the Nile rises and waters it. The land of Canaan is arid, *"and God brought us out of Egypt to give us the land of Canaan,"* the Israelites said.

However, the truth is that when God gave the children of Israel a land which was more difficult to cultivate, He was giving them the better land. Because sometimes, easier is bad and difficult is good. As the spies who went to check out the land acknowledged: *"It is a good land that the LORD our God is giving us"* (Deuteronomy 1:25).

What is so good about a difficult land?

In order to cultivate the land of Israel, much prayer would be necessary, drawing the people closer to God. Much work would be needed,

Illustration for
Hebräische Archäologie
by Immanuel Benzinger,
Jewish Encyclopedia, *1906*

making the people more humble and enhancing their connection to the land. So many good things come out of hard work and prayer. When everything is easy, and a person neglects both, his life is severely lacking. He is less happy and leads a less successful life.

So next time you feel down because of the challenges God has given you, remember that He gives challenges to those He loves. Every challenge is a chance to grow closer to God and to make something special of yourself and your life. Easier isn't always better, and sometimes our difficulties are our greatest gifts — just as the land of Israel was to God's beloved children!

Important to God: Devotion 7

FAITH IN THE PROMISE-KEEPER

ABRAM BELIEVED
THE LORD, AND HE
CREDITED IT TO HIM
AS RIGHTEOUSNESS.

— Genesis 15:6

N ext time you are at the beach, or any place with sandy soil, scoop up a handful of sand. In essence, you are holding an object lesson of God's promise to Abram. Remember the promise — *"I will surely bless you and make your descendants as numerous as the stars in the sky and as the sand on the seashore"* (Genesis 22:17)?

God didn't promise Abram wealth or more possessions or even fame. God promised Abram a nation, a people who would be so great in number that they would rival the stars in the sky or the grains of sand on the seashore. It is a promise that we Jews have held on to through thousands of years, during times of exile and persecution. It is a promise that has connected us — physically and spiritually — to our homeland, Israel.

But remember when God gave that promise to Abram? In Genesis 15, Abram had no children, no sons, and he was beginning to despair of ever having an heir. God came to Abram in a vision and comforted him; He renewed the promise given to Abram in chapter 12: *"Look up at the heavens and count the stars — if indeed you can count them ... So shall your offspring be."*

And how did Abram respond? Abram believed: *"Abram believed the LORD, and he [God] credited it to him as righteousness."* That was all that was needed. It was his belief that made Abram right with God. The fulfillment of God's promise did not rest on what Abram did — or did not do — but on Abram's faith in the One who gave the promise.

Abraham's Counsel to Sarai
by James Tissot, circa 1896 to 1902, the Jewish Museum, New York

The lesson is the same for us. We can do all the right things — go to worship, engage in Bible study, act charitably toward others — but ultimately that's not what makes us right with God. Rather, it is the combination of both our faith and our actions — our holy deeds — plus, our heartfelt confidence that God is who He says He is and that He will do what He promises, that bring us closer to God.

Faith in the Promise-Keeper and following His word are what sustained the Jewish people for centuries. They are the bedrock of our conviction that Israel is our home. Let your faith and deeds in the Promise-Keeper be the bedrock of your life as well.

THE SECRET OF IMMORTALITY

"DO NOT BE AFRAID,
JACOB MY SERVANT, FOR I
AM WITH YOU," DECLARES
THE LORD. "THOUGH I
COMPLETELY DESTROY
ALL THE NATIONS AMONG
WHICH I SCATTER YOU, I
WILL NOT COMPLETELY
DESTROY YOU."

— Jeremiah 46:28

o not be afraid, Jacob my servant, for I am with you ..." These words to the children of Israel come right after the prophet Jeremiah had prophesied that Egypt would soon fall into the hands of Babylon and her people exiled there as punishment for going to war against Israel.

Jeremiah told the Egyptians: *"Pack your belongings for exile, you who live in Egypt"* (Jeremiah 46:19) and *"'Take your positions and get ready, for the sword devours those around you'"* (46:14). Egypt was headed for disaster.

All this did little to console the people of Israel because they were slated for a sim-

Baruch Writing Jeremiah's Prophecies *by Gustave Doré, 1891, for* La Grande Bible de Tours

ilar fate. They had already been warned that they would be captured by the Babylonians. They, too, had sinned and were deserving of punishment. When the people of Israel heard Jeremiah's words, they weren't comforted; they were afraid!

This is why the prophet ends with God's words of comfort for Israel: *"Do not be afraid... Though I completely destroy all the nations among which I scatter you, I will not completely destroy you."* This is God's eternal promise to the Jewish people — He will never completely destroy them.

And even though all logic and statistics say that a tiny nation that has been expelled from its own land twice and has been persecuted for centuries should no longer exist, the nation of Israel lives. According to many theologians, the very fact that the nation of Israel exists today is proof enough of God and the veracity of the Bible.

In 1899 Mark Twain wrote:

The Egyptian, the Babylonian, and the Persian rose, filled the planet with sound and splendor, then faded to dream-stuff and passed away; the Greek and the Roman followed; and made a vast noise, and they are gone; other people have sprung up and held their torch high for a time, but it burned out, and they sit in twilight now, or have vanished. The Jew saw them all, beat them all, and is now what he always was, exhibiting no decadence, no infirmities of age, no weakening of his parts, no slowing of his energies, no dulling of his alert and aggressive mind. All things are mortal but the Jew; all other forces pass, but he remains. What is the secret of their immortality?

The source of Jewish immortality is no secret to believers. It is God Almighty. He says, *"'Pharaoh king of Egypt is only a loud noise'"* (Jeremiah 46:17), but Israel is forever.

Important to God: Devotion 9

THE SPIRIT OF YOUTH

"WHEN ISRAEL WAS
A CHILD, I LOVED HIM,
AND OUT OF EGYPT I
CALLED MY SON."

— Hosea 11:1

While the modern state of Israel may still be in its childhood, the nation of Israel is one of the oldest nations in the world. When the prophet Hosea referred to Israel's childhood, he wasn't referring to the last 70 years. He was referring to the nation's true beginning, thousands of years ago, when the children of Israel were taken out of Egypt.

About *this* stage the prophet said, *"When Israel was a child, I loved him."* But the Jewish sages teach us another way to understand the verse from the Hebrew: "Israel is a child, therefore I love him." Even today, say the sages, Israel is like a child. And that is something that God loves.

One of the profound differences between children and the elderly is the ability to recover. If a child falls down and hurts his knee, he gets up pretty quickly.

48

Even if he sheds a few tears, he is off and running again just a few minutes later. But for someone in their older years, a simple fall can result in broken bones and irreversible damage. Older people have weaker bones and need more time to heal. Children are simply more resilient.

No nation on the face of the Earth has experienced the traumas that the nation of Israel has had to deal with, repeatedly, over thousands of years. Expelled from its homeland twice, subjected to inquisitions, pogroms, holocausts, and all kinds of hostility, the nation of Israel has responded with the resilience of a child.

Though deeply bruised and beaten, Israel cannot be broken. Injuries heal quickly, and she is back on her feet. Israel continues to build and rebuild though her enemies seek to destroy her every single day. This is what the prophet meant when he called Israel a child. The nation may be old, but her spirit is young.

The lessons we can glean from Hosea's words and from the nation of Israel's experience are timeless — no matter what life throws our way, we can respond with the wisdom that comes with age, but also with the resiliency of a child as we trust and depend upon the One who loves us like a Father.

Important to God: Devotion 10

BLESSINGS FROM THE HEART

THEN AARON LIFTED HIS HANDS TOWARD THE PEOPLE AND BLESSED THEM. AND HAVING SACRIFICED THE SIN OFFERING, THE BURNT OFFERING AND THE FELLOWSHIP OFFERING, HE STEPPED DOWN.

— Leviticus 9:22

Twice a year, on the holidays of Passover and *Sukkot*, more than 30,000 worshipers crowd the Western Wall plaza as Jews from all over the world receive the priestly blessing.

In Leviticus chapter 9, the priests were assuming their role as the spiritual leaders of Israel. Today, more than 3,000 years later, many Jews can still trace their family lineage all the way back to Aaron. These priests, *kohanim* in Hebrew, recite the priestly blessing even today and bless the nation of Israel. Nothing like this has been seen on such a magnitude since the Temple was destroyed 2,000 years ago. It is quite a sight to behold!

The first time we see a priest blessing the children of Israel is Leviticus 9:22, when we read, *"Then Aaron lifted his hands toward the people and blessed them."* The Jewish sages note, that while this practice became a foundational tradition in the

Jewish faith, there is no place in the Bible where the priests are actually commanded to bless the nation.

Later, in Numbers 6, the priests were told how to bless the people: *"'This is how you are to bless the Israelites ...'"* (v. 23). They were given the words of the blessing: *"'"The LORD bless you and keep you; the LORD make his face shine on you and be gracious to you; the LORD turn his face toward you and give you peace"'"* (v. 24–26). However, the priests were never given a directive from God or Moses to bless the nation of Israel.

The sages offer an explanation for why this is so. A blessing, by its very nature, must come from the heart. In order for a blessing

Solomon Dedicates the Temple at Jerusalem
by James Tissot, circa 1896 to 1903,
the Jewish Museum, New York

to have power and influence, it must stem from a place of love, not obligation.

Friends, we in Israel cherish your blessings in every form that they come — be they in prayer, in charity, or in working on behalf of the people of Israel. We believe deeply in Genesis 12:3 where God promises: *"I will bless those who bless you ..."* However, we humbly request that as you bless Israel, you also love Israel. The greater your love for Israel, the greater your blessing will be.

Don't bless Israel because it's the right thing to do, bless Israel because it's what God has laid on your heart to do. As you bless Israel with love, may God bless you in return with His everlasting love.

*David Ben-Gurion publicly pronouncing
the Declaration of the State of Israel,
May 14 1948, Tel Aviv, Israel*

STATE OF ISRAEL

"'But I said to you, "You will possess their land; I will give it to you
as an inheritance, a land flowing with milk and honey." I am the
Lord your God, who has set you apart from the nations.'"
— Leviticus 20:24

The story of the modern state of Israel is one of the greatest stories in the history of the world. Nations rise and fall, as the Bible tells us, but never before in human history has a nation been destroyed, scattered, and reborn — not once, but twice! Though greatly outnumbered and facing the threat of destruction from Day 1, Israel won her independence in 1948 and has emerged as a beacon of democracy in an area of the world where basic freedoms for many are denied.

The story of Israel, however, goes beyond the historical. The story of Israel is a reminder to the world that God still works miracles for His chosen nation. The story of Israel is one of hope, of redemption, and of God's faithfulness to His promises that should serve as an encouragement for us all.

ISRAEL'S NOT-SO-SECRET WEAPON

IF THE LORD HAD
NOT BEEN ON OUR SIDE
WHEN PEOPLE ATTACKED
US, THEY WOULD HAVE
SWALLOWED US ALIVE
WHEN THEIR ANGER
FLARED AGAINST US …

— Psalm 124:2–3

Israel is 1/800th the size of the Arab world, most of which is bent upon destroying her. By all natural calculations, Israel should not exist. Israel should have disappeared before she even declared independence. How is it possible for such a tiny nation to survive in the midst of her enemies? It's like Daniel in the lion's den!

The truth is that Israel should have disappeared long ago, with all the other nations of the world that have come and gone, risen and fallen. No other nation on earth has been expelled from its own homeland and then survived to return to it. And Israel did it twice — once in the year 538 B.C.E., and then again, more than 2,000 years later in 1948. Israel is one big miracle!

Theologians, historians, philosophers, authors have often pondered — what is the secret to the immortality of the Jewish people? Why has this particular nation and people survived over the millennia?

The secret of the immortality of the Jews is

actually no secret at all. God says very clearly — and repeatedly in His Word — that He will preserve the Jews and bring them back to Israel. Here is just one example: *"'I am with you and will save you,' declares the LORD. 'Though I completely destroy*

Israeli soldiers in Nirim, May 15, 1948

all the nations among which I scatter you, I will not completely destroy you'" (Jeremiah 30:11).

In Psalm 124, the psalmist writes about Israel's secret weapon: God! The psalmist wrote, *"If the LORD had not been on our side when people attacked us, they would have swallowed us alive."* In every generation, someone tries to destroy the Jews, yet every time the plot is foiled. The psalmist continued, *"The snare has been broken, and we have escaped"* (v.7). Just when the Jews seem trapped and slated for

destruction, the trap is broken, and the Jews are saved. God steps in, and that's why the Jews are still here today.

Friends, when you need some inspiration or encouragement to believe that anything is possible with God, you need not look any further than Israel. If Israel can beat the odds, so can you. If Israel can receive miracles, so can you. The God of Israel can do anything, so never lose hope.

We know the secret to Israel's success, and God is your secret weapon, as well.

State of Israel: Devotion 2

DOING THE HARD WORK

Moses and Joshua bowing before the Ark *by James Tissot, gouache on board, circa 1896-1902, The Jewish Museum, New York*

"AND MAKE TWO
CHERUBIM OUT OF
HAMMERED GOLD
AT THE ENDS
OF THE COVER."
— Exodus 25:18

Thomas Edison, in 1915

Thomas Edison once said, "The three great essentials to achieve anything worthwhile are: hard work, stick-to-itive-ness, and common sense." I think that most people are OK with the "common sense" component, but when it comes to sticking with something when it gets tough or when the work is hard, many folks tend to run the other way. Hard work, after all, is just that — hard!

In chapter 25 of Exodus, we read about the instructions for the construction of the Tabernacle and the ritual objects within it. One of the objects that we come across is the cover of the Ark that contained the Ten Commandments, which was to be adorned with *cherubim*. We read, *"And make two cherubim out of hammered gold..."*

Now, translated literally from the original Hebrew, the verse reads, "And make the two golden cherubim, hammered out you shall make them …" Here's the interesting part: The word for "hammered out" in Hebrew is *miksha*, which is nearly identical to the Hebrew word for "difficult." Based on this understanding, the Jewish sages provide an alternate understanding for that phrase: "even if it is difficult, you shall do it."

By looking deeper into the multiple meanings of this phrase, the sages sought to provide us with an important life lesson: Don't run away from hard work! When called to a task, don't be intimidated by the hard work it may take to accomplish it. Most worthwhile things take hard work. Raising children is hard work; relationships are hard work; and making a contribution to society takes hard work.

When the early pioneers returned to the land of Israel in the early 1900s, a lot of hard work was involved. The Jewish people who believed in reclaiming the ancient homeland worked harder than almost anyone. They spent their days draining swamps, digging ditches, cutting stones, and laying the foundation for what would eventually become Israel's renowned agricultural accomplishments.

Their days were filled with hard physical labor, and at night, they retired in tents, often shared by three or more people. The work was harder than anything many of these immigrants previously had experienced. Yet, they persevered, and because of that, Israel is what she is today.

There are other types of hard work, which are not necessarily hard physically, but are difficult in other ways. Saying "I'm sorry" can be hard. Starting again after multiple failures is hard. Fixing a damaged relationship is hard. Accepting criticism and taking responsibility can be some of the most difficult things that we are called to do. However, just as it is in the physical realm, hard work is worth the effort. The sages teach, "the more difficult it is to do God's will, the greater the reward."

So work hard…and with joy.

State of Israel: Devotion 3

CALL ON THE NAME OF GOD

David and Goliath
by Osmar Schindler, 1888

"SOME TRUST IN
CHARIOTS AND SOME
IN HORSES, BUT WE
TRUST IN THE NAME OF
THE LORD OUR GOD.

— Psalm 20:7

Psalm 20 is among the most well-known of all psalms. In the Jewish tradition, it is part of our daily prayer service because it speaks to the various struggles that we grapple with daily. Its message is beautifully summed up in verse 7: *"Some trust in chariots and some in horses, but we trust in the name of the LORD our God."* No matter what battle we are fighting in life right now, and no matter how much things seem to be not in our favor, God can help us be victorious.

This psalm, penned by King David, is reminiscent of his very first battle when he took on the giant Goliath. Everyone tried to talk him out of fighting the giant. David was just a boy, so small that the armor King Saul offered him only weighed him down, so he went into battle unprotected — in physical armor, that is.

David came fully armored in the most impenetrable armor that exists — David came clothed in the name of God. He said to the giant Goliath, *"You come against me with sword and spear and javelin, but I come against you in the name of the LORD Almighty ..."* (1 Samuel 17:45). And with God's help, David took that giant down.

Here's another story from Israel's not-so-distant past. In spring 2003, Israel was fighting a war against terrorism. The Israel Defense Forces (IDF) were fairly successful,

F-16I "Sufa"
(photo by Maj. Ofer)

but a few battles were hard to win. One such fight took place in Jenin, a Palestinian stronghold. The Israeli fighters described an incident where the morale was very low. Many soldiers had already lost their lives, and as a last resort, an Israeli general had threatened over the loudspeaker to send in F-16 fighter jets. It was an empty threat that neither the soldiers nor the terrorists took seriously.

That is until a loud booming sound was heard moments later. At first the soldiers were confused, but then they realized the sound was thunder, even though it was spring and in Israel it *never* rains in the spring. The terrorists were not as wise. They immediately surrendered. When asked why, they said, "We heard the sound of fighter jets and knew we were defeated." God's thunder won the battle. A modern-day miracle!

What battles are you fighting today? Call on the name of God. With God on our side, we can slay any giant and overcome all adversity. No matter how big the obstacles seem, our God is bigger. No matter how mighty the enemy might seem, our God is even stronger. Let God fight your battles today — and every day — and you will be victorious.

State of Israel: Devotion 4

NO STOPPING GOD'S PLANS

Job and His Friends *by Gustave Doré*
for La Grande Bible de Tours *(1891)*

"I KNOW THAT YOU
CAN DO ALL THINGS;
NO PURPOSE OF YOURS
CAN BE THWARTED."
— Job 42:2

David Ben-Gurion, Israel's first Prime Minister, once said, "In order to be a realist in Israel, you have to believe in miracles." Perhaps he said so since he lived through one: the establishment of the state of Israel in 1948, just three years after the Nazis had murdered six million defenseless Jews. When the nation of Israel declared her independence, there was dancing in the streets. But as predicted, shortly after, there was war.

At the time, there were 600,000 Jews in the Middle East in a sea of 30 million Arabs. How could the tiny state exist with what historians would determine to be indefensible borders by human standards?

No one expected the Jewish state to last more than a few months, but Israel pushed back the coalition of Arab armies that attacked her in 1948 with nothing more than a few planes and some spirited fighters, many of them Holocaust survivors.

No one expected Israel to survive the Six-

Day War in 1967, either. Facing the mighty Egyptian army, the Jordanians, and Syrians, everyone expected a massacre. Israelis even dug mass graves in parks expecting extensive casualties. Yet, Israel won that war as well and even managed to reunite Jerusalem under Jewish sovereignty once more.

And so it was in the 1973 *Yom Kippur* War, when Israel again was outnumbered and out-gunned, and while she sustained heavy ca-sualties, Israel remained. Thus, it continues today.

No matter how many times Israel is threatened, attacked, or terrorized, the Jew-ish state remains. It exists for one reason, and for one reason only: God said so. In nu-merous places in the Bible, the prophets pre-dicted the rebirth of Israel. Just one example is Amos 9:15 where God said: *"I will plant Israel in their own land, never again to be uprooted from the land I have given them."* When God has a plan, nothing can stop it.

In the book of Job, we read: *"I know that you can do all things; no purpose of yours can be thwarted."* When God has a plan, nothing can get in the way. It is true for Israel, and it is true for the plans that God has for each and every one of us.

We waste so much energy worrying. We worry about the future; we worry about our kids, about the world, and about our old age. But stop and consider this: God has a plan. He is all-powerful, all-loving, and unstoppable. While it's true that we must put in our best effort to help create our ideal outcome, it is also true that we must leave it all in the hands of God.

Through our faith we will see miracles. We will see the culmination of God's design.

State of Israel: Devotion 5

GOD'S UNBREAKABLE WORD

Balaam and the Angel
by Gustav Jaeger, oil on canvas, 1836

"GOD IS NOT HUMAN, THAT HE SHOULD LIE, NOT A HUMAN BEING, THAT HE SHOULD CHANGE HIS MIND. DOES HE SPEAK AND THEN NOT ACT? DOES HE PROMISE AND NOT FULFILL?"

— Numbers 23:19

At some point in our lives, we all have experienced broken promises. Perhaps someone broke a promise to us that left us feeling disappointed or even betrayed. Sometimes, we might be forced to break a promise ourselves because something legitimately important came up, and we feel terrible about breaking our commitment. There is only one being who we can count on to never break His promise and that is God.

In this passage from Numbers 23, the evil sorcerer Balaam — who King Balak of Moab had hired to curse the children of Israel — discovered this truth the hard way.

First, let's take a look at some background information. According to Jewish tradition, this was not Balaam's first encounter with the children of Israel. No, Balaam had been plotting against this nation for centuries. The Jewish sages teach that Balaam was the mastermind behind the Egyptian plan to enslave the Israelites as a way of permanently subjugating them. So, as you might imagine, Balaam was more than a little disappointed when God set the Israelites free. It upset his entire plan, his greatest "accomplishment." It's no surprise then that Balaam was all too eager to curse the Israelites when asked by the king of Moab.

However, try as he might, every time that Balaam tried to curse the children of Israel, blessings came out instead. Balaam's goal was to have the Israelites die in the desert or, better yet, return to slavery in Egypt. Balaam would be vindicated, and his honor restored. However, God had already promised to bring the Israelites out of Egypt and into the Promised Land.

Balaam's Prophecy, a print from the Phillip Medhurst Collection of Bible illustrations in the possession of Revd. Philip De Vere at St. George's Court, Kidderminster, England

On his second attempt to curse the people, Balaam couldn't help but declare, "God is not human, that he should lie, not a human being, that he should change his mind. Does he speak and then not act? Does he promise and not fulfill?" In other words, Balaam, by his own unwilling admission, would not be able to change God's plan nor could he cause God to break His promise.

Let's use this teaching to remember that God does not break His promises and reflect on a few of His promises.

God promises reward for obedience: "'If you follow my decrees ... the ground will yield its crops and the trees their fruit'" (Leviticus 26:3–4). He promises to save the righteous from trouble: "and call on me in the day of trouble; I will deliver you ..." (Psalm 50:15). The Lord promises to forgive those who repent: "If my people... turn from their wicked ways, then will I hear from heaven, and I will forgive their sin..." (2 Chronicles 7:14). And God promises to bless those who bless Israel: "I will bless those who bless you ..." (Genesis 12:3).

Let's live according to God's promises. His faithfulness is assured, and His kindness is forever.

State of Israel: Devotion 6

NEVER FORGOTTEN

"CAN A MOTHER FORGET THE
BABY AT HER BREAST AND
HAVE NO COMPASSION ON
THE CHILD SHE HAS BORNE?
THOUGH SHE MAY FORGET,
I WILL NOT FORGET YOU!"
— Isaiah 49:15

Imagine being a young Jew in Europe during the late 1800s. The Holocaust has not happened yet, but pogroms, blood libels, and poverty abound. Life is tough for the Jewish people without a secure homeland. You have read the Bible and learned with the rabbis. You are told that somewhere in the Middle East there is a place for the Jews. You are told about how the Jews once flourished there until they were exiled.

You are promised that someday the Jews will return, and you pray daily for redemption. But it has been 2,000 years. For two millennia, Jews have been asking to return to their homeland, and yet, they still are in exile. Is there hope? Will it ever happen? In your darkest hours, you wonder, "Has God forgotten us?"

These verses from Isaiah 49 are traditionally read between *Tisha B'Av*, the day that commemorates a series of tragedies that have befallen the Jewish people throughout history, and the High Holy Days, beginning with *Rosh Hashanah*. Appropriately, these readings are called "The Seven Comforts." They are selections from the prophet Isaiah that speak about better times for the Jewish people, and they are designed to bring the people from the despair of *Tisha B'Av* to the salvation and redemption of *Yom Kippur*.

Isaiah 49:14, we read, *"The Lord has forsaken me, the Lord has forgotten me."* Just as the Jews must have wondered during the long exile before the miraculous rebirth of Israel, they then wondered if God had forgotten them.

Can you relate? Sometimes we pray and pray for something, and our prayers seem unanswered. When will I find a job? When will we be blessed with children? Sometimes the wait is so long that we feel forgotten. But our Father in Heaven never forgets.

The very next verse reads, *"Can a mother forget the baby at her breast?"* It's almost impossible for a mother to forget about her dear, precious child. God is just as attentive to us and more so: *"Though she may forget, I will not forget you!"* Even if those closest to us abandon us, God will never forget us. We are His children, His loved ones. We are never forgotten!

Next time you or someone you know thinks that God has forgotten them, read Isaiah 51:3, *"Joy and gladness will be found in her, thanksgiving and the sound of singing."*

After 2,000 years of waiting, God's promises have been fulfilled in our times. There is joy and singing in Jerusalem once again, just as the prophets promised. Though their wait was long, God never forgot His children, the Jewish people, and He will never, ever forget you.

State of Israel: Devotion 7

WHEN THE WALLS COME DOWN

A section of the Bar-Lev Line

THEY WILL LAY SIEGE TO ALL THE
CITIES THROUGHOUT YOUR LAND
UNTIL THE HIGH FORTIFIED WALLS
IN WHICH YOU TRUST FALL DOWN.
THEY WILL BESIEGE ALL THE CITIES
THROUGHOUT THE LAND THE
LORD YOUR GOD IS GIVING YOU.

— Deuteronomy 28:52

The Bar-Lev Line was a chain of fortifications built along the Suez Canal after the Sinai Peninsula had been taken from Egypt during the 1967 Six-Day War. Israel wanted to protect herself against the possibility of another Egyptian invasion, and so the solution was to build a $300-million wall made out of sand and concrete that was, on average, 80 feet tall and spanned about 100 miles.

The line, named after the Israeli Chief of Staff Haim Bar-Lev, was expected to keep invading forces at bay for 24 to 48 hours. However, when the day did come and the *Yom Kippur* War began, it took Anwar Sadat only two hours to break through the wall and launch an

*General Haim Bar-Lev,
photo by Paul Goldman
(1961)*

assault. When it was needed most, that great barrier, the wall of security, was useless.

66

In Deuteronomy 28, we read about the curses that will come upon the children of Israel should they disobey the Lord: *"They will lay siege to all the cities throughout your land until the high fortified walls in which you trust fall down."* Should the Israelites be disobedient, they would be attacked by enemies and thrown out of their land. The pivotal moment would come when the *"walls in which you trust fall down."* Once those walls were down, the Israelites would be vulnerable and open to attacks.

Jeremiah, the prophet who warned of the exile that would soon come to the disobedient Israelites, said: *"Cursed is the one who trusts in man, who draws strength from mere flesh . . . But blessed is the one who trusts in the LORD, whose confidence is in him"* (Jeremiah 17:5–7). Those who trust in man or anything physical are doomed. They will be let down, disappointed, defeated, and demolished. However, the one who trusts in God will be secure forever.

During the *Yom Kippur* War, after the great wall fell, after stunning defeats, and against incredible odds, the Israeli army realized that they had only one true line of defense: God. And indeed, He produced miracles, and the war was won!

Sometimes in life, God makes our walls fall down. Because it is only when we lose hope in our trusted physical and material defenses that we truly learn to trust in God.

What are the great walls in your life? Are they people whom you depend upon? Is it money in the bank? Is it a strong army or a good president? None of these are capable of protecting us or are worthy of our trust. Let us remember that it is God who fights our battles and it is He who gives us shelter — now and forevermore.

State of Israel: Devotion 8

APPRECIATING OUR PAST

Archaeological site close to City of David in Jerusalem

SO EPHRON'S FIELD IN MACHPELAH NEAR MAMRE—BOTH THE FIELD AND THE CAVE IN IT, AND ALL THE TREES WITHIN THE BORDERS OF THE FIELD—WAS DEEDED TO ABRAHAM AS HIS PROPERTY IN THE PRESENCE OF ALL THE HITTITES WHO HAD COME TO THE GATE OF THE CITY.

— Genesis 23:17–18

During the Israeli War of Independence in 1948, the Jordanians captured Jerusalem. After destroying and looting many centuries-old synagogues, they decided to build some structures of their own. They chose a site southwest of the ancient Temple to build an Islamic school. When Israeli archeologists heard of this, they quickly sent a message to the Jordanians that the site was a very important archeological site. It contained the remnants of an Islamic palace from the 7th century. The Jordanians sent an abrupt reply, "We do not care about palaces from the past. We need a school today!"

The Jewish people have always cared deeply about the past. It is from the past that we learn how to live in the present and create a better future.

In Genesis 23, we read that Abraham bought the Cave of Machpelah from Ephron the Hittite. The Jewish sages teach that each man felt that he got the better deal. Ephron received 400 shekels. For some perspective, research has uncovered that the average yearly wage at the time was six to eight shekels. Ephron made a killing! However, Abraham appreciated the priceless value of the cave since it was the burial site of Adam and Eve. As an important historical and spiritual site, the cave was beyond value to Abraham.

Burial of Sarah
by Gustave Doré

In Deuteronomy 32:7 we read, *"Remember the days of old; consider the generations long past ..."* We are required to remember history and to consider the significance of the past. It is only when we appreciate our history that we can fully live in the present.

Since the time of Abraham, the children of Israel have always honored their history and kept a record of the past. Exodus 24:7 makes reference to *"the Book of the Covenant."* The sages teach that this book contained the history of the children of Israel. When the Israelites were enslaved in Egypt, they would read from this book every week on the Sabbath. Its contents included the promise that God made to their forefather Abraham that while his descendants would go down to Egypt, they would also be redeemed.

The book also told of tests and trials that their forefathers overcame. It told of miracles and providence afforded to them by God. Reading this book of history gave the Israelites the strength, faith, and fortitude to make it through their most difficult times.

Today, we also need to remember and consider our personal histories, our family histories, the roots of our faith, and world history in general. Think of something that happened in your family's history — an inspiring story or occurrence — and draw strength from the past to guide you today.

State of Israel: Devotion 9

NO PLACE LIKE HOME

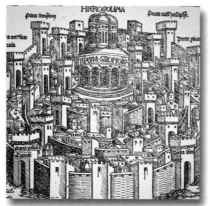

The oldest printed prospect of Jerusalem, by Hartmann Schedel, Nürnberg, 1493

IF I FORGET YOU, JERUSALEM, MAY MY RIGHT HAND FORGET ITS SKILL. MAY MY TONGUE CLING TO THE ROOF OF MY MOUTH IF I DO NOT REMEMBER YOU, IF I DO NOT CONSIDER JERUSALEM MY HIGHEST JOY.

— Psalm 137:5–6

In 1903, Joseph Chamberlain, the British Colonial Secretary, made an offer to Theodor Herzl and his Zionist group. The British were prepared to give the Jews 5,000-square miles in Uganda, Africa to serve as a Jewish homeland. The proposal evoked a fierce debate. On one hand, the land would provide the Jews with a homeland where they would be free to live in peace and protect themselves from danger.

On the other hand, it fell far short of the Zionist dream to return to the ancient homeland of the Jews — Israel. Thankfully, the offer was declined because the land was deemed unsuitable. However, the question remained: Even though the historical homeland of

Theodor Herzl, January 2, 1897, by Carl Pietzner

the Jews is Israel, does it really matter where the Jewish homeland is today?

Psalm 137 answers that question with an emphatic "Yes!" For 2,000 years, Psalm 137:5 has been a cornerstone of Jewish worship and devotion: *"If I forget you, Jerusalem, may my right hand forget its skill."* For centuries, we longed for, prayed for, and worked for the Jewish return to Jerusalem. At times of joy, this verse was read as we remembered Jerusalem. A small part of every Jewish home was left unfinished to remember the destruction of Jerusalem. Every year on the ninth day of the Hebrew month of *Av*, we spend the day fasting and crying over Jerusalem and the destruction of the Holy Temples.

Jerusalem. Not Poland, not America, and not Uganda. Jerusalem is the only capital the Jews have ever had, and Israel is the only Jewish homeland that will ever be!

This is because Israel is where the Jews belong. In Deuteronomy 1:8, God says, *"See, I have given you this land. Go in and take possession of the land the LORD swore he would give to your fathers ... and to their descendants after them."* Guess which land God was talking about? Not Uganda! The land of Israel was promised to the children of Israel and their descendants for all eternity.

In Jeremiah 50:19, God says, *"But I will bring Israel back to their own pasture, and they will graze on Carmel and Bashan; their appetite will be satisfied on the hills of Ephraim and Gilead."* Even though the Israelites would go into exile, God would bring them back. Not to New York and California, but to Carmel and Bashan in Israel. Israel is — and forever will be — our eternal homeland.

State of Israel: Devotion 10

DRY BONES

THEN HE SAID TO ME: "SON OF MAN, THESE BONES ARE THE PEOPLE OF ISRAEL. THEY SAY, 'OUR BONES ARE DRIED UP AND OUR HOPE IS GONE; WE ARE CUT OFF.' THEREFORE PROPHESY AND SAY TO THEM: 'THIS IS WHAT THE SOVEREIGN LORD SAYS: MY PEOPLE, I AM GOING TO OPEN YOUR GRAVES AND BRING YOU UP FROM THEM; I WILL BRING YOU BACK TO THE LAND OF ISRAEL."

— Ezekiel 37:11-12

Just barely a generation ago, the Jewish people found themselves standing in the ashes of the Holocaust. Over six million Jews had been murdered, nearly two million of them children, just for the crime of being a Jew. It was the worst devastation that the Jewish people had suffered in the nearly two millennium of exile, persecution, expulsion, humiliation, and assimilation.

More than one-third of the entire world Jewish population had been obliterated. Like the prophet of Ezekiel, we looked down in the valley of death, Sheol, weary and weak, and asked, "Can these dry dead bones live again?"

And behold a miracle! God breathed life into those dry bones and they came together, bone to bone, sinew to sinew. They took on flesh and spirit, and the nation lived again! As God said through the prophet, *"... these bones are the people of Israel. They say, 'Our bones are dried up and our hope is gone; we are cut off'... 'My people, I am going to open your graves and bring you up from them; I*

will bring you back to the land of Israel.'"
(Ezekiel 37:11-12).

Three years after the Holocaust and defeat of Nazi Germany, the modern nation of Israel was born. On November 29, 1947, in nothing less than a miracle, the United Nations voted to support the creation of the modern state of Israel. Opposition arose almost imme-diately, but on May 14, 1948, eight hours before the end of the British Mandate of Palestine, the Jewish state of Israel was reborn.

Child survivors of Auschwitz, January 1945

Against all odds, the Jews returned to their homeland. We didn't give up when challenged in war after war, terror, and bloodshed. Amidst inconceivable conditions and opposition, the nation of Israel not only survived, but also thrived. The land itself, which had been barren for thousands of years, began to give blossom and bloom. Hebrew, a language all but forgot-ten, was resurrected and spoken in the streets once again.

As we give gratitude to God for the miracle of modern day Israel, we recognize that God continues to be involved in the works of His world. We recognize and hold fast to the truths found in His Word —the God of Israel neither slumbers nor sleeps (Psalm 121:4); anything is possible with God (Genesis 18:14); and that nothing — be it armies, terrorists, or anti-Sem-itism — will stand in the way of His plan and purposes (Psalm 33:10).

Amen!

The Widow's Mite *by Joseph Tissot, opaque watercolor over graphite on gray wove paper, between 1886 and 1894, The Brooklyn Museum*

R RIGHTEOUS GIVING

> *"'If any of your fellow Israelites become poor and are unable to support themselves among you, help them as you would a foreigner and stranger, so they can continue to live among you.'"*
> — LEVITICUS 25:35

*E*ven before the people had stepped foot into the Promised Land, God gave His people instructions for how they were to conduct themselves and how they were to treat others. Chief among those was God's command to care for the poor and oppressed, the foreigner and the stranger, the orphan and the widow. Caring for the less fortunate is a fundamental value for both Christians and Jews.

In Judaism, however, charity is more than an act of benevolence. The word for charity, *tzedakah*, comes from two Hebrew words — *tzedek*, meaning "justice," and *kah*, a Hebrew name for God. Together, they mean the "justice of God." Giving to the poor and the needy isn't just an act of kindness; it is an act of justice and righteousness. We care about the less fortunate because it is the right thing to do.

Tzedakah is righteous giving, and God calls upon us all, Christians and Jews, to be good stewards of all He has blessed us with and care for one another. *Tzedakah* from Christians and Jews around the world has helped Israel survive and thrive until today. Through *tzedakah*, we can continue to participate in the restoration of Israel and the fulfillment of all God's prophecies.

75

Righteous Giving: Devotion 1
PAID IN FULL

BLESSED ARE THOSE
WHO HAVE REGARD FOR
THE WEAK; THE LORD
DELIVERS THEM IN TIMES
OF TROUBLE.
— Psalm 41:1

A story is told about a young man who was walking deep in the woods one hot summer day. When he became overcome with fatigue, hunger, and thirst, help wasn't so easy to find. The young man decided to knock on the first door that he saw. When he found a home, he resolved to ask for water, nothing more. A young girl opened the door, and when the young man asked for water, she brought him a large glass of milk instead. That milk gave the young man the energy he needed and bolstered his spirits so that he could make it home.

Years later, that little girl grew up and became very sick. She was sent to the city so that she could be treated by one of the nation's top doctors. As she underwent surgery, Dr. Howard Kelly recognized the patient who he was treating — it was that little girl who had been so kind to him years ago.

After the surgery, Dr. Kelly asked that all medical bills for the patient be sent to him for approval. As he looked them over, he scrawled something in black ink. When the woman re-covered and was ready to leave the hospital, she was nervous to open the final bill. When she did, she was surprised to find this note from the doctor: "Paid in full with one glass of cold milk."

In the opening line of Psalm 41, David wrote: *"Blessed are those who have regard for the weak; the LORD delivers them in times of trouble."* Those who are kind to others in their time of need will find that help comes to them when they themselves are in need.

In the *Talmud*, the Jewish sages tell a similar story about a man known as Benjamin the Righteous

Rabbi Yechiel Eckstein serves food to needy people at the Mana Hama Soup Kitchen in Ashdod, Israel, September 1, 2011

who single-handedly supported a widow and her seven sons during years of famine. Some-time later, he became very ill and was on the brink of death when angels pleaded before

God: "Is it not written that he who saves a life, saves an entire world? Is it right that a man who saved the lives of a widow and her seven sons die so young?" Immediately, God added 22 years to Benjamin's life.

In Hebrew, the word "to give," *natan*, is a palindrome. It reads the same way backward and forward in order to teach us that when we give, we also get back. May we always be motivated to give generously and live com-passionately. We can save many lives with our charity, including our own.

Righteous Giving: Devotion 2
EXTENDING ACTS OF KINDNESS

"AND IF YOU SPEND
YOURSELVES IN BEHALF OF
THE HUNGRY AND SATISFY
THE NEEDS OF THE OPPRESSED,
THEN YOUR LIGHT WILL RISE
IN THE DARKNESS, AND
YOUR NIGHT WILL BECOME
LIKE THE NOONDAY."

— Isaiah 58:10

Hillel the Elder was a great Jewish sage who lived in the Holy Land during the first century BCE. He once was challenged by a man who asked, "Teach me the entire *Torah* while I am standing on one foot!" Hillel took up the challenge and replied, "What is hateful to you, do not do to others. The rest is commentary — go study it!"

Hillel's reply was a flip-flopped version of the biblical command to *"love your neighbor as yourself"* (Leviticus 19:18). In other words, Hillel was teaching that loving others is, in essence, the entire teaching of the Bible.

With that as our framework, we can better understand the context of Isaiah 58, where God — through His prophet Isaiah — chastised the people for their meaningless fast days. Outwardly, they were serving God. However, God, who sees into everyone's heart, knew that their worship was only superficial and He wanted none of it. What God truly desired for His people — both then and now — is to stop injustice, free the oppressed, clothe the naked, feed the hungry, and provide shelter for the poor.

Kindness toward others is what God loves best.

In Psalm 118:19 we read, *"Open for me the gates of the righteous; I will enter and give thanks to the LORD."* Referencing this verse, the sages teach that when a person passes away, every person will stand in judgment. We will each be asked, "What was your occupation?" If one answers, "I fed the hungry," they will answer, "This is God's gate. You, who fed the hungry, may enter." If one answers, "I gave drink to the thirsty," they will reply, "This is God's gate. You, who gave drink to the thirsty, may enter." And so on. All who performed acts of charity and kindness will gain entrance to God's gate.

Helping others through acts of kindness has always been of utmost importance in Judaism; indeed, as the sages' teaching indicates, in the Jewish tradition, it is the way into God's Kingdom. Isaiah put it this way, *"Feed the hungry, and help those in trouble. Then your light will shine out from the darkness, and the darkness around you will be as bright as noon"* (Isaiah 58:10).

How can we honor God? By serving and helping others. As one 18th-century rabbi once put it, "The physical needs of another are my own spiritual obligation."

God counts on us to provide for the needy and to use what He has given us for the less fortunate. In that way, we show our regard for God as Creator of all people, share His goodness with others, and draw others to Him. In addition, we contribute to the overall mission of all humanity, which in the Jewish faith is known as *tikkun olam*, or "fixing the world," by making it a place of goodness and godliness.

Righteous Giving: Devotion 3

THE LORD'S SHOVEL

BE SURE TO SET ASIDE A TENTH OF ALL THAT YOUR FIELDS PRODUCE EACH YEAR.

— Deuteronomy 14:22

There is a story about an ambitious young man who told his pastor that he promised to tithe his income. Together, the pastor and the man prayed for God to bless his career. At that time, the man was making $40 a week and contributed $4 each week to the church. As time went by, the young man became increasingly successful to the point where he was tithing $500 a week. At that point, the man called up the pastor to see if he could be released from his tithing promise as it was too costly now. The pastor replied, "I don't see how you can be released from your promise, but we can ask God to reduce your income back to $40 a week, then you'd have no problem tithing $4."

God judges what we give by what we keep.

In this verse from Deuteronomy, we are commanded to give away at least 10 percent of what we earn. Jewish tradition teaches that we should give away more than that — up to 20 percent of our earnings (but no more). While that may seem difficult and counter-productive to someone trying to make ends meet, the Jewish sages offer this encouragement: Those who want to become wealthy should tithe their money! The sages add that it's impossible to become poor from giving to charity. On the contrary, they say, the more you give your money away, the more you receive.

How can that be true?

A prestigious man was once asked how he could give away so much money to charity and yet still be so wealthy, and this is what he replied: "Oh, as I shovel it out, He shovels it in, and the Lord has a much bigger shovel!"

When God sees that we use our money to help others, He blesses us with more. Our contributions are essentially our best investments. Perhaps this is what the verse in Proverbs 22 means when it says, *"A generous man will himself be blessed, for he shares his food with the poor"* (v.9). In actuality, even more than the rich man is helping the poor man, the poor man is helping the rich man — because he gives him an opportunity to help himself and earn great rewards.

Friends, we are so grateful for all the contributions that so many Christians from around the world have contributed to the many purposes of *The Fellowship*. We pray that as you bless Israel, God will bless you. We trust that, whatever you give to help others will be returned to you with the Lord's much bigger shovel — and enable you to give even more!

Righteous Giving: Devotion 4

OUR
ONLY TRUE
POSSESSIONS

Death of Korah, Dathan and Abiram
by Gustave Doré, engraving, 1865

AS SOON AS HE FINISHED SAYING ALL
THIS, THE GROUND UNDER THEM SPLIT
APART AND THE EARTH OPENED ITS
MOUTH AND SWALLOWED THEM AND
THEIR HOUSEHOLDS, AND ALL THOSE
ASSOCIATED WITH KORAH, TOGETHER
WITH THEIR POSSESSIONS.

— Numbers 16:31–32

Korah was an extremely wealthy man. Even today, the expression used in Hebrew to describe an affluent person is "as rich as Korah." The *Talmud* says that hundreds of mules were needed just to carry the keys to Korah's treasure houses. Legend has it that Korah was one of the wealthiest people to ever live.

In the book of Ecclesiastes, King Solomon writes, *"I have seen a grievous evil under the sun: wealth hoarded to the harm of its owners"* (Ecclesiastes 5:13). The Jewish sages explain that the wealth in this verse — the kind that hurts its owners — is a reference to Korah. Korah's wealth gave him a false sense of security and caused him to think that he was greater than he really was. But Korah's wealth also ended up his greatest enemy. It led to his rebellion and his downfall.

The Jewish sages teach that Korah's sons stood by his side in his rebellion. When the ground opened up, it swallowed up Korah, his sons, and all their possessions. However, the sages teach that the sons of Korah repented while they were underground, and consequentially, they were miraculously rescued.

Jewish tradition teaches that while underground, Korah's sons wrote Psalm 49, a powerful psalm about wealth that we still read today, *"Do not be overawed when others grow rich . . . for they will take nothing with them when they die, their splendor will not descend with them"* (Psalm 49:16–17).

Imagine this profound moment of clarity as Korah's sons stood in-between worlds, watching their wealthy father and his prominent supporters perish in an instant. Where was their money now? All the money in the world could not buy back even a moment of life! Their money was worthless.

A story is told about a member of the famous wealthy Rothschild family. Someone asked him, "Exactly how much wealth do you have?" In response, Lord Rothschild answered, "Let me show you." He led the man to a room and showed him many documents. They were receipts from charities that he had supported.

"These," said Lord Rothschild, "are my only true possessions. Only the money that I have given away will accompany me to the grave."

In the end, all possessions are meaningless; only our good deeds will be with us forever. So let us convert our wealth into charity and use our possessions to do kindness. Then we will have something of true value that will be with us forever.

Nathan Mayer Rothschild, 1st Baron Rothschild, from the 1901-1906, Jewish Encyclopedia

Righteous Giving: Devotion 5

THE COIN OF FIRE

"EACH ONE WHO
CROSSES OVER TO THOSE
ALREADY COUNTED IS
TO GIVE A HALF SHEKEL,
ACCORDING TO THE
SANCTUARY SHEKEL, WHICH
WEIGHS TWENTY GERAHS.
THIS HALF SHEKEL IS AN
OFFERING TO THE LORD."

— Exodus 30:13

The Jewish sages teach that when God commanded Moses that every Israelite should bring a half-shekel as part of taking the census, Moses was confused. He didn't understand the significance of a half-shekel. In response, tradition teaches, God showed Moses a half-shekel on fire, and then he understood the meaning.

Two questions: First, why was it so hard for Moses to understand what a half-shekel looked like? That doesn't seem too difficult a task! Second, why does God show him a coin on fire? What's the meaning of that?

Moses knew what a half-shekel looked like physically. He just couldn't understand what it looked like spiritually. The trouble Moses had was in understanding how such a mundane item with such little value could become holy before the Lord.

When God showed Moses the coin on fire, He was exposing its true reality. Deep inside the piece of metal were sparks of holiness, waiting to be released. When the half-shekel was used for God's purposes, the "fire" within the coin would be released and go straight up to heaven, just as the animal sacrifices did.

It wasn't the *physical* contribution that God was after; it was the *spiritual* contribution — the act of generosity on the part of the Israelites and their commitment to God's Word. When they used the half-shekel properly, its holiness was released and its potential realized.

Rabbi Elimelech, an 18th-century rabbi, added another level of meaning. He explained that fire can either be enlightening and warming, or it can be destructive and consuming. Likewise, all money has the potential for both good and evil. If used for evil causes, it can bring destruction to the individuals who spend it and many others. But when used for God's purposes, it becomes a blessing to those who

spend it and many others.

As it says in Proverbs: *"A generous person will prosper; whoever refreshes others will be refreshed"* (11:25). Giving doesn't diminish us; it makes us even stronger.

There is a deep and holy fire burning inside every coin or bill that comes our way. Let us never take this responsibility lightly or forgo the opportunity to release the "fire" and be a blessing to others. Just as the children of Israel contributed to God's purposes in Moses' time, our obligation is no different today. So make a gift of charity today and let the holy fire warm you, guide you, and bring much light into your life.

Righteous Giving: Devotion 6

GIFTS FROM THE HEART

The Erection of the Tabernacle and the Sacred Vessels
from Figures de la Bible *(1728)*

MOSES SAID TO THE WHOLE
ISRAELITE COMMUNITY, "THIS IS
WHAT THE LORD HAS COMMANDED:
FROM WHAT YOU HAVE, TAKE AN
OFFERING FOR THE LORD. EVERYONE
WHO IS WILLING IS TO BRING TO
THE LORD AN OFFERING OF GOLD,
SILVER AND BRONZE."

— Exodus 35:4–5

Most of us have been blessed with gifts from the people in our lives. Some have been expensive and others simple. Some we genuinely enjoy; others we pretended we liked. But the gifts we will always remember are the ones that were given from a place of deep love — even if it was nothing more than a handmade piece of "art" from a child in our lives. Those gifts are priceless.

In Exodus 35, we read about the construction of the Tabernacle, in Hebrew, *mishkan*, God's temporary home. The Jewish sages point out the fact that the *mishkan* was never destroyed. Unlike the two Holy Temples, which were built as permanent structures, the *mishkan* never fell into enemy hands. When it was no longer needed (because the Temple was built), it was merely disassembled and stored away. Jewish tradition teaches that it was buried deep under the Temple Mount.

How could it be that God's "permanent" home was easily destroyed, while the more vulnerable temporary house seemed invincible?

The sages credit the contributions given to the construction of the *mishkan* with its longevity. More specifically, they explain that it wasn't what was given as contributions — God only asked for something from *"what you have"* — not anything extravagant. The power was in how the gifts were given. They were given from a "willing" heart. They were contributions made with love, and consequently, the best gifts possible.

In contrast, we learn that when the First Temple was constructed, many contributions came from Huram, king of Tyre: *"So Huram finished all the work he had undertaken for King Solomon in the temple of the Lord"* (1 Kings 7:40). The sages explain that Huram's contributions were more about his own pride than his love

Solomon and the Plan for the Temple,
*illustration from a Bible card
published by the Providence
Lithograph Company, 1896*

for God. Since the Temple didn't have the same amount of love in its construction, it was weaker, so to speak, than the *mishkan*, even though its physical materials may have seemed much stronger.

The lesson we can learn about giving — both to the people in our lives and for God's purposes — is that we need to be just as attentive to *how* we give as to *what* we give. A hug given with love can be far more meaningful than a hastily bought gift card.

When we open up our wallets, we must first open up our hearts. That way, we will ensure that everything we contribute will go a long, long way and that whatever our gift makes possible will be strong and enduring. So whatever your gift is to others today, be it large or small, give it with love from a willing heart.

Righteous Giving: Devotion 7

WITH DIGNITY AND FELLOWSHIP

WHEN YOU MAKE A LOAN OF
ANY KIND TO YOUR NEIGHBOR,
DO NOT GO INTO THEIR HOUSE
TO GET WHAT IS OFFERED TO YOU
AS A PLEDGE. STAY OUTSIDE AND
LET THE NEIGHBOR TO WHOM
YOU ARE MAKING THE LOAN
BRING THE PLEDGE OUT TO YOU.

— Deuteronomy 24:10–11

Not all giving is the same. While the act of making a financial donation might look the same on the outside, what's on the inside of the giver makes all the difference.

Some giving comes with strings attached, where the giver expects something in return from the recipient. In those instances, the recipient is made to feel that he or she "owes" their benefactor, be it exaggerated honor, total compliance, or something else. Then there is giving with feelings of judgment and disparagement of the recipient. While these feelings might not be put into words, attitude can still be felt deeply by the recipient.

Finally, there is giving with generosity and love. The giver expects nothing in return from the recipient. This is giving with dignity where the benefactor doesn't diminish the beneficiary, but honors and respects the person regardless of his or her situation. These sentiments can also be sensed by the recipient even if they are not expressed vocally.

In these verses from Deuteronomy 24, God makes it clear that He wants us to give to others in a way that helps the recipient without diminishing his or her dignity. Among the laws laid down in chapter, Scripture teaches that when a person gives a loan to a person, he or she may not enter the home of the recipient in order to collect the collateral. Rather, the person receiving the loan must bring the collateral out to the lender.

Such delicate sensitivity protects the dignity of the person receiving the loan. The *Torah* continues and explains that if the item of collateral is the borrower's coat, the lender must return it at night if the borrower is poor, so that he or she will not go to sleep cold. Again, we are encouraged to help the person in a truly thoughtful manner.

With so many ways to give to others, it is essential that we get it right. This is why when *The Fellowship* launched our program to help Israel's needy elderly, many of whom are Holocaust survivors, we called the program *With Dignity and Fellowship*. Giving the project such a title underscores our goal of helping the elderly in a way that provides them not just physical assistance, but also revives their soul. Financial aid is accompanied by companionship. Assistance is provided with honor and respect. The recipients are given a chance to share as well — their stories, their wisdom, and their fellowship.

Next time we offer assistance to someone, let's pay attention to how we give. Are we giving without judgment? Do we have unspoken expectations? When we are generous and respectful in our giving, we can revitalize a person in crisis — both body and soul.

Righteous Giving: Devotion 8

GIVE TO LIVE

"THE PRIEST WHO IS
ANOINTED AND ORDAINED
TO SUCCEED HIS FATHER AS
HIGH PRIEST IS TO MAKE
ATONEMENT. HE IS TO PUT ON
THE SACRED LINEN GARMENTS
AND MAKE ATONEMENT FOR
THE MOST HOLY PLACE, FOR
THE TENT OF MEETING AND
THE ALTAR, AND FOR THE
PRIESTS AND ALL THE MEMBERS
OF THE COMMUNITY."

— Leviticus 16:32–33

T he central part of the *Yom Kippur* service is missing today. Chapter 16 of Leviticus is dedicated to the description and instructions for the *Yom Kippur* service that was performed when the Tabernacle and later the Temples stood. Today, we no longer have a high priest, nor do we participate in ritual sacrifices. So how do we achieve atonement?

There are three keys that take the place of the sacrificial service performed in biblical times. Together, they unlock the doors of heaven and allow us to sweeten any harsh decrees, or even to remove bad decrees altogether. The three components are: repentance, prayer, and charity.

It's easy to understand why repentance and prayer can help change things for the better, but why is charity singled out as one of the three components? In fact, the Jewish sages teach that charity is so powerful that it can save a person from death! What is so extraordinary about giving charity?

A story is told about the great sage Akiva who lived during the time when the Second Temple was destroyed. The story goes that Akiva was on a ship when he caught sight of another ship going down. He knew a great *Torah* scholar who was on that ship and assumed that he had drowned. Later on, Akiva came across that scholar and was astounded that he was alive. "How did you survive?" Akiva asked him. "It must have been your prayers," the man replied. "I was tossed from wave to wave until I found myself on the shore."

Akiva ben Joseph,
unknown artist, 1568

Not satisfied, Akiva pressed, "Was there some great deed that you did before you boarded the ship?" The man explained, "Well, there was a beggar who approached me as I was boarding the ship and I gave him my loaf of bread. He thanked me and said, 'Just as you have saved my life, may God save yours.'" At that moment, Rabbi Akiva understood the great merit of charity and proclaimed Ecclesiastes 11:1: *"Cast your bread upon the waters, For you will find it after many days"* (NKJV).

When we give another person a lifesaving gift, the life we are saving just might be our own. How we treat others is how God will treat us. This explains why when we give charity on *Yom Kippur*, as is the Jewish custom, we have the power to overturn any non-favorable judgments set against us.

Remember that charity can come in different forms, not just monetary. We can donate our time and our talents to God's purposes as well. As we give life and joy to others, may God bless us with life and joy as well.

Righteous Giving: Devotion 9

DON'T HOLD BACK

DO NOT WITHHOLD
GOOD FROM THOSE
TO WHOM IT IS DUE,
WHEN IT IS IN YOUR
POWER TO ACT.

— Proverbs 3:27

Judaism tells a cautionary tale about charity — more specifically, about *withholding* charity. There was a wealthy Jewish businessman who consistently gave charity to a Jewish poor man. For years, the poor man would show up at the rich man's home and leave with enough money to support his family.

One day, after the poor man made one of his regular visits, the wealthy man grew resentful and thought it was unfair that he had to support this poor man. It was his money after all — what right did the poor man have to expect a monthly handout?

The next time the poor man showed up at his door, the wealthy man informed him that he would not be giving him charity any longer. Despondent, the poor man went back to his family empty-handed. But, as God would have it, suddenly the poor man's floundering business began to boom. In a short while he was earning more than enough money.

At the same time, the wealthy man experienced a turn in his fortune as well — but not for the good. His business suffered huge losses, and the once wealthy man found himself barely getting by. The distraught formerly wealthy man went to see his rabbi to ask why he experienced such a steep loss. The rabbi explained that the wealthy man had been entrusted by God with the poor

Be'er Sova Soup Kitchen food preparation, 2011

man's money. It was his job to distribute it. Since he didn't want the job, God took the money away and gave it directly to the poor man himself.

In Proverbs 3:27, we read: *"Do not withhold good from those to whom it is due, when it is in your power to act."* In Hebrew, the word used to mean "charity" is the word *tzedakah*. However, the Jewish sages point out that "charity" is an insufficient translation of the word *tzedakah*. The word *tzedakah* comes from the word *tzedek* which means "justice." A more accurate definition would be "righteousness."

According to Judaism, when we give charity we are not being kind; we are being just. We are returning to the poor person what is rightfully his and what God has given us to steward. This is why Proverbs cautions us against withholding what we have to give; it isn't ours to begin with!

In Deuteronomy 15:10 we learn, *"Give generously to them and do so without a grudging heart."* If we think our money is ours, it can lead to resentful giving. But when we recognize that all we have is from God in order to use for His purposes, we can give generously and with love, grateful for the opportunity to be God's partner, a lender and not a borrower.

Righteous Giving: Devotion 10

HEAVEN ISN'T FAR AWAY

WHOEVER IS KIND
TO THE POOR LENDS
TO THE LORD AND HE
WILL REWARD THEM
FOR WHAT THEY
HAVE DONE.
— Proverbs 19:17

There is a Jewish folktale set in the early 19th century in Eastern Europe about a Hassidic rabbi and his dedication to charity. One day a skeptic arrived in the rabbi's city to see for himself this rabbi and what the fuss was all about. Every Friday morning, the rabbi would simply disappear. He wasn't in the synagogue or his home. The skeptic asked the rabbi's followers where their leader went. They replied, "Where else but to heaven? The people of the town need peace, sustenance, and health. Surely our rabbi is in heaven pleading our cause."

The skeptic decided to find out for himself. One Thursday night he hid himself in the rabbi's house. Before dawn, he heard the rabbi emerge from his bedroom dressed as a peasant. Then the rabbi pulled out an axe and began to chop wood outside in the darkness. The rabbi brought the wood to a run-down cottage, not knowing anyone was following him.

When he got to the door of the house, the rabbi knocked on the door. An old, poor, and ill woman opened the door. The disguised rabbi explained that he had cheap wood to sell her so that she would be warm for the winter. "But I have no money," the woman replied. "I will give it to you on credit," the rabbi said. "But how will I repay

you?" the woman wondered. "God will find a way to see that I am repaid," answered the rabbi. "But who will light the fire; I am too ill," the woman protested. "I will" said the rabbi, and he did.

After witnessing all this, the skeptical man decided to become a disciple of this particular rabbi. When he would hear other followers explain that their rabbi went to heaven on Friday mornings, he would add "and even a little higher."

The story teaches us the importance of giving charity and its centrality in the Jewish tradition. In Proverbs we read, *"Whoever is kind to the poor lends to the Lord, and he will reward them for what they have done."* Giving charity is tantamount to lending to God. God gives us the opportunity to do Him a favor! Of course, God could supply everyone with all their needs on His own, but He allows us to help Him in helping others and rewards us for our kindness as well.

Friends, let's take advantage of the opportunity God has given to us to become part of His plan in making the world a better place. Heaven isn't that far away. It's a place wherever kindness abounds, and it can be found around the corner, across the globe, or right inside your own home.

A ALIYAH

He will raise a banner for the nations and gather the exiles of Israel; he will assemble the scattered people of Judah from the four quarters of the earth.
— ISAIAH 11:12

We cannot tell the story of Israel, from biblical times to today, without talking about *aliyah*. It is a Hebrew word meaning "ascent," and in biblical time, it referred mainly to the pilgrimages made to Jerusalem three times a year on the holy days of *Pesach* (Passover), *Shavuot* (Pentecost), and *Sukkot* (The Feast of the Tabernacle.) As Jerusalem was set atop a hill, the worshipers literally had to ascend to the Holy Temple.

Today, we say use the term *aliyah* to refer to the millions of Jews who have returned to their eternal home, Israel, from the four corners of the world where they had been exiled nearly 2,000 years ago. Today, we are witnesses to prophecy being fulfilled, to God's promises being realized, and to a people being redeemed. Even more miraculous is that *aliyah* is being made possible through the generosity and support of Christians around the world, as Isaiah prophesied, *"This is what the Sovereign LORD says: 'See, I will beckon to the Gentiles, I will lift up my banner to the peoples; they will bring your sons in their arms and carry your daughters on their hips'"* (Isaiah 49:22).

Aliyah: Devotion 1

ON WINGS OF EAGLES

Yemenite Jews en route to Israel from Aden, Yemen. In the course of the Operation Magic Carpet (1949-1950), the entire community of Yemenite Jews (called Teimanim, about 49,000) immigrated to Israel.

"YOU YOURSELVES HAVE
SEEN WHAT I DID TO
EGYPT, AND HOW I CARRIED
YOU ON EAGLES' WINGS AND
BROUGHT YOU TO MYSELF."

— Exodus 19:4

Between June 1949 and September 1950, Israel ran a secret operation known as Operation Magic Carpet. During that time, 380 flights were made between Yemen and Israel, rescuing more than 49,000 Jews from Arab countries where they were being oppressed.

When the Jews being rescued boarded the planes that would airlift them to Israel, they were sure that the messiah had come. They had never seen planes before, and to them, these were the "eagles" prophesied about in the book of Isaiah: *"They will soar on wings like eagles"* (Isaiah 40:31). To the Jews of Yemen, those airplanes were God's eagles that would carry them home. And that's how Operation Magic Carpet became more popularly known as Operation Wings of Eagles.

The Jews of Yemen weren't completely wrong. Although they were still waiting for the messiah, they were experiencing the miracles foretold by the prophets. The Jewish people were on their way home, and like eagles, they took flight.

The children of Israel who left Egypt for Israel also went on *"eagles' wings."* In these verses from Exodus chapter 19, God told them, *"You yourselves have seen what I did to Egypt, and how I carried you on eagles' wings and brought you to myself."* The children of Israel cer-

tainly didn't fly on airplanes, so just what did God mean?

The Jewish sages explain that all other birds carry their young in their claws because they are afraid of the high-flying predators that soar above them. But no bird flies higher than the eagle. The eagle only has to worry about men below. So it puts its young on its wings so that the eagle itself comes between its young and any danger. If anyone wants to take a shot from below, they will have to deal with the eagle first.

Like an eagle, no one is higher than God. And like an eagle, He protects His children with love. When God took the children of Israel out of Egypt, He placed the "Pillar of Cloud" between them and the Egyptians. The Egyptians would have to get through the cloud if they wanted to reach the Israelites. But God would not let them. He miraculously kept them safe from harm.

Today, God continues to bring His people back to their ancient homeland. And He continues to do this *"on wings of eagles"* — with miracles, compassion, and love. Here at *The Fellowship* we are part of that miracle, together with our Christian friends around the world. Our aptly named ministry, *On Wings of Eagles*, helps needy and persecuted Jews around the world come home to Israel and create a new life.

We invite you to join us in the fulfillment of this ancient prophecy unfolding in our times. Together we can help those eagles take flight!

Aliyah: Devotion 2

"ONE BY ONE"

Jewish Agency representatives meeting Yemenite immigrants, upon arrival at the Lod Airport, October 23, 1949 (photo by Théodore Brauner)

IN THAT DAY
THE LORD WILL
THRESH FROM THE
FLOWING EUPHRATES
TO THE WADI OF EGYPT,
AND YOU, ISRAEL,
WILL BE GATHERED
UP ONE BY ONE.

— Isaiah 27:12

At the dawn of World War II in 1939, there were almost 17 million Jews in the world. In 1945, that number had shrunk to 11 million. Today, the Jewish people have rebuilt and grown, yet the number of Jews worldwide stands between 13 million and 14 million, not even close to the Jewish population before its decimation at the hands of the Nazis.

However, not all the news is bleak. In the 1920s, less than 100,000 Jews lived in Israel, then called Palestine. The Jewish state was not yet recognized, and the Jews who lived there were subject to oppression. Today, there are almost six million Jews living and thriving in Israel, where they are free to worship as they please and are defended by one of the world's greatest armies.

The fact that there are so many Jews living in Israel today is the fulfillment of ancient biblical proph-

esies. God promised that the day would come when His people would return home. However, this is only the begin-  ning. Most Jews, more than seven million of them, still live outside of Israel. Many live in places like the former Soviet Union, where they live in poverty, or in Middle Eastern countries, where they live under oppression.

God gives us the opportunity to play a role in fulfilling His purposes, and today we are able to help bring His people home.

This reminds me of the story about a young starfish-thrower. One day, a man was walking along a beach at dawn when he noticed a boy picking up starfish and flinging them into the sea. "Why are you doing this?" he asked. "Because if they aren't back in the sea when the sun comes up, they'll die," the boy answered. "Don't you realize that the beach goes on for miles?" the man said. "How will your efforts make any difference?" The boy looked at the starfish in his hand and threw it into the sea. Then he said, "It made a difference to that one."

This verse from Isaiah is one of many biblical prophecies about the Jews returning to their homeland. This time, the prophet Isaiah emphasized that they will come back *"one by one."* This teaches us that we don't have to throw our hands up in despair when we take on the giant task of helping all the Jewish people return home. We just need to help them one by one, until everyone is home.

A Yemenite family walking through the desert to a reception camp set up by the "Joint" near Aden (photo by Zoltan Kluger, November 1, 1949), National Photo Collection of Israel, Photography dept. Government Press Office

Aliyah: Devotion 3

AGAINST ALL ODDS

*Hungarian Jews not selected as laborers,
photo from the Auschwitz Album, May 1944*

"'YET IN SPITE OF THIS,
WHEN THEY ARE IN THE LAND
OF THEIR ENEMIES, I WILL
NOT REJECT THEM OR ABHOR
THEM SO AS TO DESTROY
THEM COMPLETELY, BREAKING
MY COVENANT WITH THEM.
I AM THE LORD THEIR GOD.'"

— Leviticus 26:44

Recently I met an elderly woman who is receiving assistance from *The Fellowship*. As she told me her life's story, I realized that she was a living, breathing miracle. By all accounts, she should not be here. It doesn't make sense that Olga is alive today or that she is living in Jerusalem.

The first miracle is that Olga's parents met. Olga's father was the only one of his family, including his first wife, to survive a Nazi roundup and mass killing. Olga's mother was miraculously saved from a brutal Nazi concentration camp. The two met and married in a ghetto in Russia. Shortly afterward, Olga was born.

The second miracle came when Olga was just a few months old. The ghetto was bombed, and Olga was wounded. Bleeding and screaming, Olga's mother whisked her into hiding with the other Jews, but her mother was forced to leave because Olga's screaming would give them away to the Nazis. Olga's mother took refuge in an abandoned house where she fully expected to be captured. However, the soldiers of the allied armies found the pair and took care of Olga and her mother.

Finally, the third miracle to occur is that Olga survived at all. As an infant, Olga had been diagnosed with tuberculosis and typhus. At the time, the doctors gave her little chance to survive. And yet, Olga grew up to be healthy; she married, had children, and is now living in the land of her ancestors — the land of Israel.

As I met with this remarkable woman and reflected on her life's journey, it occurred to me that Olga's story is a reflection of the story of all Jews. By all accounts, we should not be here. No other country in history has been exiled from its land and returned to it. The Jews did it twice! Every other nation has risen, fallen, and disappeared. The normal course of an exiled nation is to assimilate and disappear. And yet, the Jews have survived 2,000 years of exile, persecution, and hardship. We are still alive, and we have returned to our ancestral homeland.

Only one explanation remains for our survival: God Almighty — in these verses from Leviticus — promised that while the nation of Israel would be punished and exiled for disobedience, He would not allow us to be utterly destroyed. It says in Proverbs: *"Many are the plans in a person's heart, but it is the LORD's purpose that prevails"* (19:21). The Lord's plan will come to pass — for the Jewish people and for all people of faith.

Aliyah: Devotion 4

THE SECOND EXODUS

Ukraine Aliyah, Freedom Flight 0001,
December 22, 2014

"DO NOT BE AFRAID, FOR I AM
WITH YOU; I WILL BRING YOUR
CHILDREN FROM THE EAST AND
GATHER YOU FROM THE WEST. I WILL
SAY TO THE NORTH, 'GIVE THEM UP!'
AND TO THE SOUTH, 'DO NOT HOLD
THEM BACK.' BRING MY SONS FROM
AFAR AND MY DAUGHTERS FROM
THE ENDS OF THE EARTH."

— Isaiah 43:5–6

In addressing the Provisional State Council in Tel Aviv eight hours before the end of British rule in Palestine, David Ben-Gurion declared the establishment of the state of Israel based on "the historic right of the Jewish people in the Land of Israel" and the "natural right of the Jewish people to be masters of their own fate."

These ringing words of Jewish independence would find their truest expression in a law passed two years later, The Law of Return. This law, which guarantees the right of all Jews to immigrate to Israel, put into practice the Zionist movement's desire to build a safe haven for all Jews. Since that law was enacted, more than 3 million Jews have returned to Israel.

But for many Jews, immigration to Israel, or *aliyah*, is more than just a legal enactment or realization of a political movement. It is the fulfillment of biblical prophecy and God's promise to the descendants of the patriarchs, Abraham, Isaac, and Jacob.

"*Aliyah* is the heart, the very ideal of Israel.

The state of Israel is only a tool, you can say, a technical tool to bring Jewish people, who have been scattered all over the world for thousands of year, back to the Holy Land," said Natan Sharansky, an Israeli politician and activist, who has been instrumental in bringing Jews back to Israel since 1988.

Natan Sharansky, on February 11, 2016, photo by Nathan Roi

Supporting *aliyah* has been at the heart of *The Fellowship* as well. We began *On Wings of Eagles*, our ministry to bring needy Jews from around the world to Israel, in 1990 when the 74-year reign of Communism ended with the collapse of the Soviet Union. At that time the door to freedom opened for one of the most oppressed groups of people on earth — Soviet Jews, who long had been denied permission to return to Israel, their biblical homeland.

Throughout the years, the scope of *On Wings of Eagles* has expanded beyond the former Soviet Union to help fund *aliyah* for Jews suffering the effects of poverty and anti-Semitism in Ethiopia, Arab nations, India, South America, France, and other countries. For centuries, Jews dreamed they would one day return to their homeland of Israel. It has been a recurring theme in our prayers recited every day, three times a day; our holiday services on Passover and *Yom Kippur* traditionally conclude with the words "Next year in Jerusalem."

Today, this is taking place before our very eyes. By praying and supporting this "second exodus" of Jews from oppression to freedom, Christians can show their compassion and concern for the Jewish people, and help fulfill the biblical prophecies that promise the return to Israel of Jewish exiles from the four corners of the earth.

Aliyah: Devotion 5

FULFILLING THE IMPOSSIBLE

A Jewish wedding in Galicia *by M. Strayamsky, traditional nissu'in in Eastern Europe during the 19th century*

"SING, BARREN WOMAN, YOU WHO NEVER BORE A CHILD; BURST INTO SONG, SHOUT FOR JOY, YOU WHO WERE NEVER IN LABOR; BECAUSE MORE ARE THE CHILDREN OF THE DESOLATE WOMAN THAN OF HER WHO HAS A HUSBAND," SAYS THE LORD

— Isaiah 54:1

Weddings are always special. However, whenever I am blessed to attend a wedding in Jerusalem, I am particularly overwhelmed with emotions and joy. This is because a wedding in Jerusalem is not just a demonstration of the love between a couple and their commitments to each other; it is also a demonstration of God's love for His people and His commitment to fulfilling the promises that He made long ago.

Recently, I attended a wedding that had a magnificent view of Jerusalem in the background. Underneath the wedding canopy stood the groom and his family. The groom was a Yemenite Jew. His grandparents and parents were forced to leave Yemen after the state of Israel was declared a nation and all the Arab countries around her declared war on all Jews. Then the bride walked down the aisle flanked by her parents. Her grandparents were Holocaust survivors who had moved to England after the war; her parents had moved to Israel when she was young.

As these two souls came together in matrimony, the significance went way beyond their individual lives. I could hear the words of the blessing we say on holidays and special occasions echoing in my mind: "Blessed are You, Lord our God, King of the universe, who  has kept us alive, and sustained us, and enabled us to reach this moment ...." So many miracles, over so many centuries, had brought us to that moment!

We read in the book of Genesis about Sarah: *"Now Sarai was childless because she was not able to conceive"* (Genesis 11:30). These verses in Isaiah similarly begin, *"Sing, barren woman, you who never bore a child ... because more are the children of the desolate woman than of her who has a husband ..."* Though Sarai (who was later called Sarah by God) was barren, God would keep His promise and she would become the mother of a great nation. Similarly, in this chapter in Isaiah, God was speaking to Jerusalem, who seemed barren and alone. God promised Jerusalem that she would once again be the home of a great nation. In both cases, and always, God kept His promises.

According to Jewish tradition, Sarah was not physically capable of having children and the birth of Isaac was a complete miracle. Yet, however unlikely it seemed, it happened because God said it would.

Let us be strengthened and inspired as we watch the fulfillment of God's promises before our very eyes. If a barren woman can become the mother of many, and the Jewish people can return to their homeland, what is possible for you?

Aliyah: Devotion 6

TWO BECOME ONE

Joseph Converses With Judah, His Brother, *by James Tissot and Followers, circa 1896-1902, The Jewish Museum, New York*

"SON OF MAN, TAKE A STICK OF WOOD AND WRITE ON IT, 'BELONGING TO JUDAH AND THE ISRAELITES ASSOCIATED WITH HIM.' THEN TAKE ANOTHER STICK OF WOOD, AND WRITE ON IT, 'BELONGING TO JOSEPH (THAT IS, TO EPHRAIM) AND ALL THE ISRAELITES ASSOCIATED WITH HIM.' JOIN THEM TOGETHER INTO ONE STICK SO THAT THEY WILL BECOME ONE IN YOUR HAND."

— Ezekiel 37:16-17

Our verses today reference the tumultuous confrontation between Joseph and his brother Judah back in Genesis chapter 44. God told the prophet Ezekiel to take two sticks of wood and write Judah's name on one and Joseph's name on the other. Then, miraculously, the two separate sticks became one.

What is the meaning of this display?

Jewish tradition teaches that the stick of Joseph represents the Diaspora (exiled) Jews while the stick of Judah represents the Jews of Israel.

Joseph, who spent most of his life exiled in Egypt, typifies Jews living outside their homeland. He was at the mercy of the Egyptians and unfairly imprisoned. But Joseph also be-

came an integral part of Egyptian society and brought blessings to the land. At the same time, he had to play it safe and make sure that he was always in good standing with Pharaoh because everything could change at any second. When Joseph's brothers came to Egypt, they didn't even recognize him because he dressed, spoke, and looked like an Egyptian.

On the other hand, Judah, who was the leader of the other brothers, spent most of his life in the land of Israel. He represents the Israeli Jews — free to live how they wanted to live, unapologetic, and strong. From Judah comes the Davidic dynasty, which represents the Jewish nation in all its strength and glory. While the Jews of the Diaspora were always characterized as weak, vulnerable, and pitiful, the Jews of Israel are seen as self-sufficient and proud.

Throughout history, there has always been these two types of Jews — and there always will be. The meaning of Ezekiel's sticks is that at the End of Days, these two types of Jews will become one. God says, *"I will take the Israelites out of the nations where they have gone. I will gather them from all around and bring them back into their own land"* (Ezekiel 37:21). God promises that He will bring His people back to Israel, and there, they will be one nation, with one king and one God.

At a welcoming ceremony for immigrants coming to Israel I recently attended, a member of the *Knesset* (Israel's parliament) got up and said that all immigrants who come to Israel bring something good with them from their former home. Whether they come from Russia, Yemen, India, America, or Ethiopia, each group brings something unique from that culture. The result is a beautiful mosaic in which all of these shades of color are made into one stunning picture.

Aliyah: Devotion 7

AN ETERNAL BOND

*Jews from the Former Soviet Union
returning to Israel in the early 1990s*

"THIS IS WHAT THE LORD
SAYS: 'IF I HAVE NOT MADE
MY COVENANT WITH DAY
AND NIGHT AND ESTABLISHED
THE LAWS OF HEAVEN AND
EARTH, THEN I WILL REJECT
THE DESCENDANTS OF
JACOB AND DAVID ...'"

— Jeremiah 33:25–26

At *The Fellowship*, we recently celebrated the 10,000th immigrant we have assisted in coming home to Israel since we began operating our own global *aliyah* (immigration) program in late 2014. Historically, with support from our Christian and Jewish donors worldwide, *The Fellowship* has helped to bring nearly 750,000 immigrants to the Holy Land.

For these immigrants, and all who arrived in the Holy Land on a daily basis, it is a dream come true. Many were saved from a war-torn country where they had been displaced from their homes and thrust into poverty. Others have been rescued from persecution and anti-Semitism. Whatever the reason, all have returned to the Jewish homeland with a promise of a brighter tomorrow. It is the fulfillment of the biblical promise in Isaiah 11:12 in which God vowed to *"assemble the scattered people of Judah from the four quarters of the earth."*

In the book of Exodus, we read about the covenant between Israel and God established at the foot of Mount Sinai. In Exodus 24:7–8, Moses oversaw the sealing of the covenant:

"Then he took the Book of the Covenant and read it to the people. They responded,

Moses Presenting the
Ten Commandments
by Julius Schnorr von Carolsfeld, 1860

'We will do everything the LORD has said; we will obey.' Moses then took the blood, sprinkled it on the people and said, 'This is the blood of the covenant that the LORD has made with you ...'"

Our verses from Jeremiah affirm that this was, is, and will always be an eternal covenant. This wasn't a deal that could be broken. This wasn't an arrangement where God might change His mind at some later date in time. God's covenant with the children of Israel is binding forever. We read in Jeremiah 33:25, *"If I have not made my covenant with day and night and established the laws of heaven and*

earth, then I will reject the descendants of Jacob and David ..."

What's God saying? That just as there will always be day and night, heaven and earth, there will always be God and the children of Israel. God established physical laws in the world, and He also created spiritual laws in the world. One of those laws is that the children of Israel will always be God's chosen people, and when the time is right, God will bring them back to Israel and *"have compassion on them"* (Jeremiah 33:26).

God promises to bring His children home no matter what. It doesn't say that God will bring them back to Israel when they deserve it; it says that God will bring them back out of compassion for them. And the most amazing part of this is that God allows *us* to help fulfill His plan by supporting these efforts to bring His children home!

Aliyah: Devotion 8

A CLOUD OR A DOVE?

"WHO ARE THESE
THAT FLY ALONG
LIKE CLOUDS,
LIKE DOVES TO
THEIR NESTS?"
— Isaiah 60:8

The book of Isaiah is filled with amazing prophecies about the messianic era, including the return of the Jewish people to Israel. But not all Jews will return in the same way. Some will come out of love and with great joy. Others will be pushed there, some against their will. The prophet Isaiah put it this way: *"Who are these that fly along like clouds, like doves to their nests?"* (Isaiah 60:8).

Tradition teaches that this verse is referring to two different sets of people. There are those who will come to Israel like clouds — they will be pushed there by the storms of anti-Semitism and war. Then there are those who will go *"like doves to their nests."* They will come of their own volition and a desire to return home. These fortunate ones won't be running away from something bad — they will be running toward something good.

Like many of the messianic prophecies in the book of Isaiah, the return of the Jewish people to their homeland has come to pass in our days. And just as Isaiah foretold, the in-gathering of the exiles has come about in these two different ways.

Jews around the world have found ref-uge in Israel, many of them arriving just after World War II when they were shut out from most of the world. Today, Israel continues to be the destination for Jews escaping oppression in countries around the Mid-dle East, Africa, and

Buchenwald survivors arrive in Haifa to be arrested by the British, July 15, 1945 from To the Promised Land *by Uri Dan p.58*

even some parts of Europe. But these are not the only Jews immigrating to Israel and it is not the only function of the Jewish state. Israel is far more than a life-raft for Jews in danger.

The state of Israel also is the living man-ifestation of a 2,000-year-old dream for the Jewish people to return to their ancient homeland. Today, Jews from all four cor-ners of the earth, including the most affluent countries in the world, are choosing to leave everything behind in order to begin again in a new land because Israel is where a Jew belongs. Israel is home.

You don't need to be Jewish to have a promised land. Every-one has an ideal place that they can get to in their lifetime, and it is more likely a spiritual space than a physical one. And they will get there in one of two ways. Some people will be pushed there by the storms in life, or some can choose to go peacefully on their own.

I know which I prefer. How about you?

Aliyah: Devotion 9

PARTNERS WITH ZION

Reverend William Hechler

"AND IN ANY LOCALITY
WHERE SURVIVORS MAY NOW
BE LIVING, THE PEOPLE ARE TO
PROVIDE THEM WITH SILVER
AND GOLD, WITH GOODS
AND LIVESTOCK, AND WITH
FREEWILL OFFERINGS FOR THE
TEMPLE OF GOD IN JERUSALEM."

— Ezra 1:4

Theodor Herzl was the father of the modern state of Israel. Like many great men, he kept a diary. Herzl recorded the journey that he underwent trying to birth the state of Israel into being, and he spoke about those who helped him along the way. One name, in particular, is mentioned more than any other in the entire account.

That name is Reverend William Henry Hechler. The greatest ally of the Jewish journalist from Vienna was an English minister. Hechler's partnership with Herzl played a fundamental role in the re-establishment of the state of Israel and the return of the Jews to their homeland.

Partnership between Jews and Gentiles for the sake of Israel goes back thousands of years to biblical times. The book of Ezra opens with a monumental declaration by Cyrus, King of Persia. Seventy years after the Jewish nation had been exiled from their homeland by the Babylonians, the Persians had taken control and initiated the Jewish return to their land. Not only did Cyrus grant permission for the return

Cyrus the Great and the Hebrews, *circa 1470*

and rebuilding of the Temple, he also urged local residents to donate to the cause. It was with the help of these Gentile friends that the Jewish people were able to return to their homeland.

Sound familiar?

The time that we are living in today shares many similarities with the time period in which Ezra lived. While his generation saw the first people in history to re-establish a homeland after being exiled from it, today's generation is witnessing the only nation in history to return to its homeland twice! And just as the initial return to Israel was only possible because of the partnership between Jews and Gentiles, today's return to Zion is also the product of a Jewish and non-Jewish alliance once again.

I don't think that's an accident. God wants to give all people a chance to be involved in the rebuilding of the Holy Land. Israel may be the homeland of the Jewish people, but Israel is for everyone. The Holy Land contains everyone's past and also their future. The Scripture tells us that the third and final temple will be a house of prayer for all nations. It is only fitting that every nation should have the opportunity to contribute to its making.

We are witnessing the fulfillment of ancient prophecies before our very eyes! The children of Israel are returning to their land, and you can become a part of it through prayer, through visits, through your voice, and your support of *The Fellowship*'s many programs and ministries.

Aliyah: Devotion 10

THE "SIX KNOCKS OF GOD"

Frederick II (the Great), King of Prussia, aged 68, by Anton Graff, 1781

HE WILL RAISE A BANNER FOR THE NATIONS AND GATHER THE EXILES OF ISRAEL; HE WILL ASSEMBLE THE SCATTERED PEOPLE OF JUDAH FROM THE FOUR QUARTERS OF THE EARTH.

— Isaiah 11:12

When Fredrick the Great asked his trusted advisor for the single, strongest piece of evidence that proved the existence of God, the advisor answered him: "The Jews, Sir, the Jews."

How is it that the Jewish people are a living testimony to the existence of God?

The answer is that the Jewish people, according to all reason and logic, should no longer exist. It is statistically impossible for such a small nation, persecuted and kicked out of land after land, to still be around. Even more unbelievable is that fact that the Jews have returned to their homeland. There is no natural explanation for the existence of Israel today, only a supernatural one. There is only one possible explanation for the survival and revival of the Jews: God.

If the Jews exist today, it is only because God exists eternally.

If the Jews were a large and mighty nation, we may have been able to attribute their perseverance to their significant numbers or military prowess. If the Jews had remained safely in their homeland since its inception over three thousand years ago, we might have been able to credit their existence today with the stability that they enjoyed throughout history. However, the Jews have enjoyed none of these advantages. They have been a small nation, less than 1% of all humanity, with neither a military nor a homeland until recent times. Under these circumstances, no nation could possibly survive.

Even more startling is that the Bible predicted these dire circumstances: *"The LORD will scatter you among the peoples, and only a few of you will survive ..."* (Deuteronomy 4:27). But the Bible also promised the miraculous return of the Jewish people: *"... he will assemble the scattered people of Judah from the four quarters of the earth"* (Isaiah 11:12). Who could make such an outrageous claims other than the Master of the world? Only God could predict and arrange such events!

In his brilliant work, "My Beloved Knocks,"

Rabbi Joseph Soloveitchik, an American rabbi who died in 1991, listed the "six knocks of God" on our doors in these times — the six

Rabbi Joseph Soloveitchik of Yeshiva University

modern miracles regarding the Jews, including the return to the land of Israel, the miracles of the Israeli army, and the establishment of the state of Israel. These supernatural events predicted in the Bible, said the rabbi, are God knocking on our door beckoning us to wake up and let Him into our lives.

We are living in wondrous times. The promises of the Bible are being fulfilled today. Let us be inspired by the miracles unfolding before our very eyes. Let us reaffirm our faith and renew our commitments to God. God is eternally faithful; may we be faithful to Him for all eternity!

Esther by *Edwin Long, 1878,*
National Gallery of Victoria, Melbourne

EDUCATE

Guide me in your truth and teach me, for you are God
my Savior, and my hope is in you all day long.
— PSALM 25:5

Israel has long fought for her right to exist — from biblical times through today. The state of Israel is a testament to the blood and tears shed by many for the right to live in our eternal homeland. Yet, one of the most insidious battles Israel continues to fight on a daily basis is the battle for truth. Our enemies, whose sole objective is to destroy the Jewish state, conduct an ongoing campaign to denigrate Israel before the world. At times, it feels like we are losing the battle.

Yet, in recent years, Israel and the Jewish people have found new friends among Bible-believing Christians, who are armed with the truth and choose to stand alongside us. Today, more than ever, we need Christians to educate themselves and others about the truth and be willing to speak out against such lies, to stand up for what might not be popular, but for what is right and true. In every generation, we have faced enemies; in every generation, we have needed Esthers to stand up and speak out *"for such a time as this"* (Esther 4:14).

Educate: Devotion 1

HEAR OUR CRIES

Moses Laid Amid the Flags
by James Tissot and Followers, circa 1896-1902,
The Jewish Museum, New York

SHE OPENED IT AND
SAW THE BABY. HE WAS
CRYING, AND SHE FELT
SORRY FOR HIM. "THIS
IS ONE OF THE HEBREW
BABIES," SHE SAID.

— Exodus 2:6

In Exodus chapter 2, we read about the birth of Moses, the one chosen by God to eventually save all Israel. As most of us familiar with the story know, the birth and survival of Moses was no easy thing. Pharaoh had decreed that every Jewish baby boy be drowned in the Nile. According to Jewish tradition, God caused a miracle (the first of many), and Moses was born three months early. This bought his parents some time, and they were able to hide Moses for three months before the time of his arrival was expected. At that point, Moses's parents realized that they had to let him go and rely on the grace of God, so they placed him in a basket, set it on the Nile River, and prayed for the best.

God arranged that just as the basket was floating on the river, Pharaoh's daughter went down to the Nile for a bath. Now follow closely. When she saw the basket, *"She opened it and saw the baby. He was crying, and she felt sorry for him. 'This is one of the Hebrew babies,' she said"* (Exodus 2:6).

The Jewish sages ask two questions: First, how did Pharaoh's daughter know that the baby was a Hebrew? Secondly, in the original Hebrew, the verse first refers to a "baby boy" in the basket, but then refers to a "youth" who is crying. Why is Moses first called a baby, but then a child?

The answer given by the sages is that the verse is speaking about two different boys. Pharaoh's daughter opened the basket and saw baby Moses. Then she saw a child — Aaron, the brother of Moses — and he was crying. She realized that Aaron was the baby's brother and understood that this was a Hebrew baby in danger of death. It was Aaron's cries that opened her heart and caused her to have compassion on Moses and save him.

Jocheved, Miriam, and Moses, *in the 1897* Bible Pictures and What They Teach Us *by Charles Foster*

The message of this teaching is that when we cry for ourselves, we have a limited effect. But when we cry for one another, we have a greater effect and can evoke miraculous salvation.

Today, I think that this message takes on an even greater meaning. When Jews cry for themselves, the world hardly listens. Yet again Jews are slaughtered. Yet again Jews are persecuted. The world yawns and moves on.

But when our Christian brothers and sisters cry out to the world on our behalf, suddenly the world listens. We need your cries today more than ever. Cry out for your Jewish brothers and sisters who face starvation, persecution, and terror. Tear open the heart of an indifferent world. Evoke their compassion.

THE HERD MENTALITY

"IF THE OFFERING
IS A BURNT OFFERING
FROM THE FLOCK, FROM
EITHER THE SHEEP OR
THE GOATS, YOU ARE TO
OFFER A MALE WITHOUT
DEFECT."
— Leviticus 1:10

Several years ago, a Christian blogger named Veronica Partridge caused quite a stir. She wrote a controversial post that had been shared more than 100,000 times and earned her an appearance on "Good Morning America." What was the contentious topic that brought Partridge into the spotlight? She wrote a piece about why she chose to give up wearing tight-fitting pants.

Partridge described how the conviction weighed heavily on her heart for a long time before she made her decision. After a conversation with some friends and corroboration from her husband that such tight-fitting pants were a stumbling block for most men, Partridge decided to forgo such clothing. She believed that dressing more discreetly was a way to honor her husband and God.

Now, whether we agree with Partridge's conviction is not the point. The point is that she took a stand for God against the mostly negative feedback that she received and the widely accepted values of today's society. But if we are truly God-centered people, we will base our behaviors on what God deems acceptable and not upon the whims of fluctuating societal norms.

In this first chapter of Leviticus, we learn about the ritual sacrifices that were brought into the Tabernacle and the Temple. Scripture lists different types of sacrifices that were brought, and the Jewish sages delve extensively into the meaning and symbolism of each type of sacrifice. One sacrifice that was brought *"is a burnt offering from the flock, from either the sheep or the goats ..."*

The sages explain that these animals represented the herd instinct — the tendency to follow the crowd because everyone else is doing so. The message for us today is that we need to sacrifice our tendency to follow the flock and instead follow only God. We need to burn up the desire to conform and become inspired to inform. We need to stand up and speak the truth even if we are standing alone.

It has been said that when the herd is running toward the cliff, the one running in the opposite direction is the one that looks crazy. When we take a stand for what we know to be right, we might look crazy to others around us who have chosen to follow the crowd. However, our interest has to be in how we look in the eyes of God, not in the eyes of people.

Great men and women such as Abraham, Moses, Esther, and countless others became great because they were brave enough to stand alone. Know that when we stand apart for what is right, we are never really alone. We are in the company of history's finest individuals.

LIES THAT HURT; WORDS THAT HEAL

SAVE ME, LORD, FROM LYING LIPS AND FROM DECEITFUL TONGUES.

— Psalm 120:2

P salm 120 is the first of 15 psalms called "Songs of Ascent." One reason these psalms are given this title is because they are especially conducive to lifting a person up from hopelessness and helplessness into knowing that anything is possible with God. Through reciting these psalms a person ascends, rising above circumstances and coming closer to God.

In this particular psalm, King David voiced concerns over the lies that were spoken about him. Like David, the Jewish people have often been the target of slander and lies designed to hurt, if not destroy them. Whether it was the countless blood libels spread in Europe, claiming that Jews used the blood of innocent Christians in baking Passover *matzot*, or lies spread by Arab propaganda designed to convince the world that Israel intentionally kills children — Israel has been the victim of lies repeatedly. Like David, we pray, *"Save me, LORD, from lying lips."*

In this psalm, David likened lies to *"a*

warrior's sharp arrows" (v. 4). The Jewish sages explain that just as an arrow was designed to kill from afar, so, too, false words can bring danger to those at a distance from the speaker. No wonder David turned to God for help! How else could he protect himself from these sharp arrows pointed in his direction?

Appropriately, this psalm is often read when Israel is in imminent danger. The last verse especially resonates with every Israeli, every Jew, and every lover of Zion. David wrote: *"I am for peace; but when I speak, they are for war"* (v. 7).

The Psalmist David Repents *by Julius Schnorr von Carolsfeld, 1860*

Israel has only ever wanted peace. While our enemies pretend to want peace as well, they have proven repeatedly that they want nothing less than the complete destruction of Israel; indeed, *"they are for war."* When our enemies saw that they could not defeat us militarily, they resorted to the age-old anti-Semitic tactic of telling lies. This is their warfare — and so much of today's media is quick to spread this deceit as truth. This is how they try to defeat us. Who can protect Israel from such vicious lies?

The answer, of course, is God. One day the truth will become clear, and until that time, God will protect His people.

But we need to do our part. Whether it's calling attention to doctored pictures or blatant lies, we need to uncover the truth and spread it. With today's technology, it's easier than ever to learn the truth and share it.

Our enemies may use their words to harm, but we can use our words to heal. We can use our words to speak the truth and, most importantly, to pray. Pray for the safety of Israel and protection from all destructive lies.

Educate: Devotion 4

SPEAK UP IN LOVE

SPEAK UP FOR THOSE
WHO CANNOT SPEAK
FOR THEMSELVES,
FOR THE RIGHTS
OF ALL WHO
ARE DESTITUTE.
— Proverbs 31:8

More than 30 years ago as a newly ordained rabbi, I was sent by the Anti-Defamation League to raise community support to protest a proposed march of a neo-Nazi group in Skokie, Illinois, a Chicago suburb where a large number of Holocaust survivors lived. Do you know who were the most willing to stand against this march? The Christian community. Why? Because of their love for the Jewish people and their sense of responsibility to stand against anti-Semitism.

One of the best ways to combat anti-Semitism — or any form of prejudice — is with love. A loving attitude toward others ensures that you will think the best of them and treat them well. If you *"love your neighbor as yourself"* you will not *"seek revenge or bear a grudge"* (Leviticus 19:18). But what if you don't harbor any ill thoughts toward others, but you encounter someone who does? Again, love is the best response.

Oftentimes, a loving but straightforward reply is all that is needed. People might not realize that what they have said is offensive unless someone tells them. And sometimes people will stop speaking hatefully if they know that such remarks do not gain them approval. Leviticus 19:17 reminds us to *"Rebuke your neighbor frankly so you will not share in their guilt."* But why would we share in the guilt of someone else who harbored anti-Semitic attitudes?

By doing nothing to stop it, we bear the responsibility. God said that if you do not warn a wicked man *"or speak out to dissuade them from their evil ways ... I will hold you accountable*

Yellow badge Star of David called "Judenstern." Part of the exhibition in the Jewish Museum Westphalia, Dorsten, Germany. The wording is the German word for Jew (Jude), written in mock-Hebrew script.

for their blood" (Ezekiel 3:18).

The Bible says to *"speak up for those who cannot speak for themselves"* (Proverbs 31:8). When you hear someone speak hatefully, you can speak up in love. There may not be anyone else present to speak up for people being verbally attacked, so we may be the only ones to speak up on their behalf.

It may be difficult or uncomfortable to speak up against hatred, and it may take some courage. But it is our God-given duty to defend those who cannot defend themselves. If we all made a loving, but firm response to anti-Semitism, we could make great strides toward eliminating this harmful attitude.

Educate: Devotion 5

NO GREATER LOVE

Esther Accusing Haman, *in*
Doré's English Bible *by Gustave Doré, 1866*

"FOR IF YOU REMAIN SILENT AT
THIS TIME, RELIEF AND DELIVERANCE
FOR THE JEWS WILL ARISE FROM
ANOTHER PLACE, BUT YOU AND YOUR
FATHER'S FAMILY WILL PERISH. AND
WHO KNOWS BUT THAT YOU HAVE
COME TO YOUR ROYAL POSITION
FOR SUCH A TIME AS THIS?"

— Esther 4:14

The account of Queen Esther is among one of the most stirring and beautiful portrayals of courage and the willingness to take a stand against evil in the Bible. Perhaps you are familiar with the story. After uncovering a plot to kill all the Jews in the country, her Uncle Mordecai pleaded with Esther to intervene on behalf of the Jews before her husband, King Xerxes.

Esther was faced with a difficult choice.

If she refused to say anything, the Jewish people would surely perish. If she did speak up, however, she risked death, since entering the king's presence without being called for could mean death. Who can forget Esther's inspiring words, as she made her decision: *"I will go to the king, even though it is against the law. And if I perish, I perish"* (v. 16).

Both Mordecai and Esther recognized that they had been placed in a unique position to save the Jewish people. They could have walked away from it. They could have decided to save themselves. But they saw they had an opportunity to make a difference, and they seized the moment and acted.

During another time in history when the Jews once again faced annihilation, there were individuals, groups, and even an entire village who recognized that they had an opportunity to make a difference — and they seized the moment and acted. We call these brave souls the "Righteous Gentiles," non-Jews, who risked their lives to save Jews during the Holocaust.

These men and women, many of whom were Christians, rescued Jews by offering them a place to hide, providing them with false papers and identities, smuggling and assisting Jews to escape, and saving children. And they often paid for their heroism with their lives.

Many of these people humbly denied that they were acting heroically. The people of Le Chambon-sur-Lignon, a Protestant village in southern France, offered a haven for Jews fleeing from the Nazis. Under the leadership of their pastor, André Trocmé, and his wife, Magda, the people of Le Chambon acted on their conviction that it was their duty to help their "neighbors" in need.

"Things had to be done, and we happened to be there to do them. It was the most natural thing in the world to help these people," the Chambonais said.

Their story, and countless others of those who stepped forward, offers powerful affirmation of their biblically mandated duty to stand up for their brethren. Indeed, as Jesus taught, *"Greater love has no one than this: to lay down one's life for one's friends"* (John 15:13).

We may never be asked to put our lives on the line in the way that Esther, or the Righteous Gentiles, did, but we can make a commitment to stand against injustice, anti-Semitism, and prejudice in our own communities. I pray that we will have the insight to see the opportunities where we can make a difference and the courage to seize the moment and act.

Educate: Devotion 6

SPEAK ON JERUSALEM

Roman triumphal procession with spoils from the Temple,
depicted on the inside wall of the Arch of Titus in Rome

SPEAK TENDERLY TO JERUSALEM,
AND PROCLAIM TO HER THAT
HER HARD SERVICE HAS BEEN
COMPLETED, THAT HER SIN HAS
BEEN PAID FOR, THAT SHE HAS
RECEIVED FROM THE LORD'S HAND
DOUBLE FOR ALL HER SINS.

— Isaiah 40:2

These verses from Isaiah chapter 40 are traditionally read following the Jewish observance of *Tisha B'Av*, on which we mourn the destruction of the Temple in Jerusalem and all other tragedies. They are part of a series of *Torah* readings called "The Seven Comforts," and as the name suggests, all contain messages of comfort and encouragement for the nation of Israel.

Appropriately, chapter 40 begins, *"Comfort, comfort my people, says your God"* (Isaiah 40:1). The next verse begins, *"Speak tenderly to Jerusalem ..."* However, the literal translation of the original Hebrew actually reads, "Speak on (the heart of) Jerusalem."

Is this a grammatical mistake? In Hebrew, the words "to" and "on" are nearly identical, and indeed, most understand this verse as speaking to Jerusalem, not on Jerusalem. However, we can learn an extremely important and relevant lesson by taking the words at face value.

Perhaps the prophet is encouraging us to speak about Jerusalem, "on Jerusalem." Let Jerusalem and Israel be the topic of conversation. Let us spread the truth about Israel as well as the needs of Israel. In this way, we comfort God's people greatly.

I can't tell you how many times I have spoken to individuals receiving aid from *The Fellowship* who have said these words to me, "Christians around the world know about us? They care about us? They are providing us with this support?"

So many Jews in Israel, and around the world for that matter, are shocked to know that they are the topic of conversation and concern for many Christians. Their initial surprise melts into comfort and gratitude. Especially in Israel, where much of the world attempts to isolate

and vilify us, it is extremely comforting to this war-torn nation to know that there are those who care about us, who stand up for Israel, who provide lifesaving aid to Israel, and who speak the truth about Israel. Sometimes I am left wondering which was the greater gift — the physical support provided by *The Fellowship* or the emotional gift that comes in the form of a virtual hug from a stranger across the globe?

Friends, I invite you to join us in fulfilling the words from the prophet Isaiah. Together, we can comfort God's people. Let's talk about the inhabitants of Jerusalem and Israel who need our help at this time. Let's pray for the peace of Jerusalem and let's speak up for Jerusalem, letting it be known that she is, and always will be, the eternal capital of the Jewish state.

The Prophet Isaiah (Isaiah 1:1-7, 16-31),
in Doré's English Bible
by Gustave Doré, 1866

Educate: Devotion 7

FOR ZION'S SAKE

The destruction of the Temple of Jerusalem
by Francesco Hayez, 1867

FOR ZION'S SAKE I WILL NOT
KEEP SILENT, FOR JERUSALEM'S
SAKE I WILL NOT REMAIN
QUIET, TILL HER VINDICATION
SHINES OUT LIKE THE DAWN,
HER SALVATION LIKE
A BLAZING TORCH.

— Isaiah 62:1

Chloe Valdary is an unlikely Zionist activist. She is a young college student from New Orleans where organized events on campus against Israel are the norm. Chloe isn't Jewish and she has never been to Israel, but Chloe is a Christian and is devoted to the Bible. She believes that Israel rightfully belongs to the Jewish people and sees a world full of lies about the conflict in the Holy Land.

Chloe also believes that it is her duty to spread the truth; not just to believe it, but also to act upon it. She began an on-campus group called "Allies for Israel" and has become a spokesperson on behalf of Israel and the Jewish people. Chloe says, "I have just one question... How dedicated are you, indeed, are we, to the maxim of 'never again?'"

Today's verses are from the final reading of the "The Seven Comforts" — those seven messages of hope and encouragement that the Jewish people traditionally read following the observance of *Tisha B'Av*, an observance marking the destruction of both the First and Second Temple in Jerusalem, and other tragedies that have occurred on the same day.

In this week's reading, we come across this famous quote from the prophet Isaiah: *"For Zion's sake I will not keep silent, for Jerusalem's sake I will not remain quiet ..."* This has become the basis of the actions of so many of Israel's dearest friends. This is the impetus behind initiatives like Chloe's and others who are doing all they can to spread the truth about Israel. It is also the source of great comfort for the Jewish people. For a people who have been persecuted and alienated for millennia, it is deeply comforting to know that we are no longer alone.

As Chloe Valdary writes, "A feeling is merely that if there is no action that follows it. Reflection and action are two things that are rendered worthless if one is not accompanied by the other." It is not enough to love Israel in our hearts. We need to love Israel and the people of Israel with our hands and with our voices.

Israel needs friends now more than ever. She needs people who are willing to stand up even if they are standing alone. People who are willing to speak the truth even if their voices are shaking. People who are willing to write, speak, and teach the truth about Israel *"till her vindication shines out like the dawn, her salvation like a blazing torch"* (Isaiah 62:1).

There is a great healing going on between the Christian and Jewish communities. Israel is strengthened and comforted by the help of her Christian friends, and we are proud to play a major role in building bridges between the two faiths at *The Fellowship.* Please join us in blessing the Jewish people both in deeds and with words.

For Israel's sake, do not remain silent. The world was silent once; let us say with Chloe and others, "Never again!"

Stones from the Western Wall of the Temple Mount, knocked down by Roman battering rams in 70 C.E. Photo by Wilson44691, May 27, 2009

Educate: Devotion 8

FOR SUCH A TIME

The Aged Simeon *by James Tissot and Followers, circa 1896-1902, The Brooklyn Museum*

"A SON HONORS HIS FATHER, AND A
SLAVE HIS MASTER. IF I AM A FATHER,
WHERE IS THE HONOR DUE ME?
IF I AM A MASTER, WHERE IS THE
RESPECT DUE ME?" SAYS THE LORD
ALMIGHTY. "IT IS YOU PRIESTS WHO
SHOW CONTEMPT FOR MY NAME.
BUT YOU ASK, 'HOW HAVE WE SHOWN
CONTEMPT FOR YOUR NAME?'"

— Malachi 1:6

Both Jews and Christians believe in the coming of the Messiah. All of us eagerly anticipate that time when there will be peace on earth and the world will be filled with knowledge of God and love for our Creator. I once heard a prominent rabbi say, "The Messiah is not delayed because of the bad people in the world. He's not coming because of the good people — good people who aren't doing their jobs."

We, who know better, must be better. If we are fortunate enough to know God and to know His Word, it is our duty to make the world a better place.

In these verses from Malachi chapter 1, God scolded Israel, specifically the priests, whose chief responsibility was to serve God. God accused the priests of having contempt for their position, *"By saying that the LORD's table is contemptible"* (Malachi 1:7).

The priests were given a special role to play in the service of God and in bringing God's people closer to Him, but they despised their roles. They took no joy in their positions and did a less than satisfactory job. What a huge insult to God who had given them such positions in the first place.

I am reminded of a verse from the book of Esther. As you may remember, Esther was chosen to be the Queen of Persia and she wielded a considerable amount of power. However, when her Uncle Mordecai came to her and requested she intervene on behalf of the Jewish people who had been condemned to death by the evil Haman, Esther hesitated.

Maybe she would be killed for trying to change the king's mind; maybe she would lose her position. But Mordecai reminded her with some of the most powerful words ever written: *"And who knows but that you have come to your royal position for such a time as this?"* (Esther 4:14). In other words, "If God has placed you in a position to further His purposes, you must do so! That's probably why

you were given that position in the first place!"

Friends, we who know and love the Bible are God's servants, His priests who have the ability to enlighten the world and bring people closer to Him. This is the time, and this is the place. Wherever God has placed you, you need to serve Him in that role. If you have political influence, use it. If you have wealth, share it. If you have an audience, speak out *"for such a time as this."*

Malachi, *watercolor circa 1896–1902 by James Tissot*

135

BE THE EXCEPTION

Return of the Spies from the Land of Promise,
(Numbers 13) *by Gustave Doré*

"NO ONE FROM THIS EVIL GENERATION SHALL SEE THE GOOD LAND I SWORE TO GIVE YOUR ANCESTORS, EXCEPT CALEB SON OF JEPHUNNEH. HE WILL SEE IT, AND I WILL GIVE HIM AND HIS DESCENDANTS THE LAND HE SET HIS FEET ON, BECAUSE HE FOLLOWED THE LORD WHOLEHEARTEDLY."

— Deuteronomy 1:35–36

A test was once conducted where 10 high school students were placed in one room and shown three lines of varying lengths. The students were told to raise their hands when the instructor pointed to the longest line. In reality, only one student was being tested. Nine of the students had been instructed beforehand to raise their hands when the instructor pointed to the second longest line. Seventy-five percent of the time, the students being tested retracted the right answer when they saw that no one else agreed with them. The researchers concluded that most people would rather be popular than be right.

It's not easy to hold firm to our convictions. It's far easier to follow the crowd.

In Deuteronomy chapter 1, Moses was speaking about Caleb, one of the 12 spies sent to scout out the land of Canaan. Moses recalled how most of the spies gave a bad report about God's chosen land and how the people rebelled against God as a result. The Israelites were punished for this act of disobedience and failure to trust God with a decree that none of them would enter the land.

However, there was one exception. Moses recounted God's decision: *"No one from this evil generation shall see the good land I swore to give your ancestors, except Caleb son of Jephunneh. He will see it, and I will give him and his descendants the land he set his feet on, because he followed the LORD wholehearted-ly."* While the nation rebelled, Caleb was the only one to stand against the crowd and urge the people to trust God and enter the Promised Land. Because of his courageous stand, he received exceptional treatment.

Truth be told, Joshua also chose to stand against the other 10 spies and side with Caleb. However, it was Caleb who spoke out first; Caleb who stuck out his neck for the sake of God. The Bible tells us, *"Then Caleb silenced the people before Moses and said, 'We should go up and take possession of the land, for we can certainly do it'"* (Numbers 13:30). Caleb dared to go against the crowd and was bold enough to stand up for God.

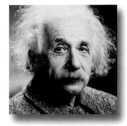

Albert Einstein in 1947

Albert Einstein once said, "The one who follows the crowd will usually get no further than the crowd. The one who walks alone is likely to find himself in places no one has ever been."

Let's be like Caleb and dare to walk alone when necessary. Stand with Israel, when the rest of the world stands against her. Bring a good report about Israel, when the rest of the world concocts a bad one. Stand with God, and stand for the truth.

THE ETERNAL JEWISH HOMELAND

Jacob's Body Is Taken to Egypt by James Tissot, circa 1896-1902, The Jewish Museum, New York

WHEN THE TIME DREW NEAR FOR ISRAEL TO DIE, HE CALLED FOR HIS SON JOSEPH AND SAID TO HIM, "... DO NOT BURY ME IN EGYPT, BUT WHEN I REST WITH MY FATHERS, CARRY ME OUT OF EGYPT AND BURY ME WHERE THEY ARE BURIED." "I WILL DO AS YOU SAY," HE SAID.

— Genesis 47:29–30

On Jewish Heritage Day 2010, a rabbi got more than he bargained for when he interviewed renowned senior journalist and then member of the White House press corps, Helen Thomas. She made remarks caught on camera that sent shock waves through the world and her own personal life. Ms. Thomas said that the Jews should "get the hell out of Palestine" and "go home to Germany and Poland."

Ms. Thomas' remarks were not just anti-Semitic and bigoted; they were a gross misrepresentation of history revealing that she was either enormously ignorant or re-writing the past. Her condemnable words cost Ms. Thomas her job, her prestigious reputation, and put an indelible black mark on her otherwise illustrious career.

Ms. Thomas' remarks were shocking, especially since they had come from a woman who was supposedly knowledgeable, having reported on the region for decades. However, she was certainly not alone in her sentiments.

There are millions who believe that the Jews should "go home to Germany and Poland," places where millions of Jews were murdered just decades ago.

But even if those two "homes" weren't places of oppression for the Jews today, that still wouldn't change the fact that the Jewish people have only had one capital and one home for generations upon generations. That place is Israel, and our capital is, was, and always will be, Jerusalem.

In Genesis chapter 47, Jacob, or Israel as he was renamed by God (Genesis 32:28), was on his deathbed. He had spent the last 17 years of his life with his family in Egypt. Yet, before his death, Jacob made his son Joseph swear that he would bury him not in Egypt, but in Israel.

The Jewish sages point out that this would not have been easy for Joseph to arrange. Aside from the travel logistics, Joseph would also have come across extreme resistance from Pharaoh. "Egypt isn't good enough for you Jews? What an insult!"

Why was it so important for Jacob to be buried in Israel? Later on, Joseph was buried in Egypt and asked that when the Jews left that they simply take him with them. Why wasn't that enough for Jacob? The sages explain that Jacob foresaw that because his children were so comfortable in Egypt they could easily forget that Israel was their true home.

Even today, just 30 minutes south of Jerusalem, we can visit the Cave of Machpelah (Tomb of the Patriarchs) where Jacob is buried. It remains an everlasting testimony to the fact that, despite what the Helen Thomases of the world might say, Israel is home to the children of Israel. It always has been and it always will be. Those of us who know this must tirelessly share this truth with the world.

LOVE YOUR NEIGHBOR

"'Do not seek revenge or bear a grudge against anyone among your people, but love your neighbor as yourself. I am the LORD.'"
— LEVITICUS 19:18

hen asked by a religious expert about the greatest commandment in the Law, Jesus replied, *"'Love the Lord your God with all your heart and with all your soul and with all your mind.' This is the first and greatest commandment. And the second is like it: 'Love your neighbor as yourself'"* (Matthew 22:37-39). Jesus, a Jew, was quoting from the *Torah*, and it is only fitting that our final key to Israel is this core value shared by Christians and Jews — loving God and loving our neighbor.

As we learn from both the Jewish and Christian Bibles, our neighbor is anyone we meet who is in need — whether they live next door, across town, or across the globe. For Christians and Jews, the call to love others is the way to bring about reconciliation — between one another and between ourselves and God. In Judaism, we call that *tikkun olam*, or "fixing the world."

Together, it is our purpose and our calling. As we share one another's burdens, as we reach out across the many years of animosity and mistrust, we will build bridges of understanding and demonstrate to the world that our faith is alive, and that our God is faithful.

Love Your Neighbor: Devotion 1

SEE THE SUFFERING OF OTHERS

FOR THIS COMMAND
IS A LAMP, THIS
TEACHING IS A LIGHT,
AND CORRECTION AND
INSTRUCTION ARE
THE WAY TO LIFE …
— Proverbs 6:23

What would you do if you saw a boy about 10 years old, looking dirty and ragged, rummaging through a garbage bin on a public street? Would you stop and ask him if he is all right? Would you take the time to care? Would you be willing to take actions that might help the boy?

This is what the New Zealand Police Force asked the public in a video they released earlier this year. The short clip featured a young actor who played the part of a homeless child looking for food in the trash. The project was a social experiment to see how people would react — or more precisely — *not* react to the poor boy's plight.

The camera captures dozens of well-dressed people walking past the child without saying a word. Some passersby approached the boy, but only to throw away trash in the bins he was sorting through. One person even appeared to take a picture of the child with his smartphone. Eventually, three school-aged young women were the only ones to stop and ask about the boy's welfare, offering him food and money.

Sadly, the overwhelming majority completely ignored this obviously tragic situation.

In the Exodus story in the Bible, we read about the ten plagues that God, through Moses, brought upon Egypt before they agreed to let the Israelites go. The ninth plague was the plague of darkness. Scripture reads:  *"So Moses stretched out his hand toward the sky, and total darkness covered all Egypt for three days. No one could see anyone else ..."* (Exodus 10:22–23).

Commenting on this verse, one prominent 19th-century rabbi taught, "The worst darkness is when a person does not want to see his suffering brother and to extend to him support." This was the true darkness of Egypt — even before the plague began. They could not see the suffering of the Israelites. They turned a blind eye to the pain of others.

In contrast, we learn in Proverbs 6:23: *"For this command is a lamp, this teaching is a light ..."* Solomon was comparing God's Word to light. Just as darkness blinds us to the suffering of others, the goal of the *Torah* is to open our eyes to the needs of others. The Bible teaches us that all people are created in the image of God. Scripture directs us to love our neighbor as ourselves. The way of God is the way of light — of seeing the suffering of others and helping where we can.

What will we do if we see someone struggling today? Will we turn the other way? Or will we be the exception to the rule, lighting the way with empathy, generosity, and love? The choice is ours.

Love Your Neighbor: Devotion 2
THE SECRET TO LOVE

**"DO NOT SEEK
REVENGE OR BEAR
A GRUDGE AGAINST
ANYONE AMONG YOUR
PEOPLE, BUT LOVE YOUR
NEIGHBOR AS YOURSELF.
I AM THE LORD."**
— Leviticus 19:18

There is a story about a rabbi who wanted to teach his students about love. That particular day, the school was serving fish for lunch. The rabbi approached a group of students who were enjoying their lunch and asked, "Do you love the fish?" "I love it!" came one boy's enthusiastic reply. "No you don't!" boomed the rabbi's voice. "If you really loved the fish, you wouldn't be eating it."

In our Scripture from Leviticus chapter 19, we come across one of the most fundamental axioms of the Bible: *"Love your neighbor as yourself."* This ideal was deemed so important that when the saintly Rabbi Akiva (first century) was asked to relay the entire Bible while standing on one foot, that phrase was his reply.

In the Christian Bible, Jesus quoted this verse from the *Torah* when asked what was the greatest commandment: *"'Love the Lord your God with all your heart and with all your soul and with all your mind.' This is the first and greatest commandment. And the second is like it: 'Love your neighbor as yourself'"* (Matthew 22:37-39).

Now, most of us are blessed with many people in our lives who make keeping this commandment very easy. But then there are those other people — you know the ones. They are the people God places in our lives who make keeping this commandment extremely challenging. How are we to love those who make loving them so difficult?

The Jewish sages let us in on a secret about love, which is actually hidden within the Hebrew word for love, *ahava*. At the center of the word *ahava* is the Hebrew word *hav*, which means "giving." Giving forms the very root of the word "love," and the sages teach that it is also the root of the act of love.

You see, we don't love those most from whom we receive; we love those most to whom we give. Just look at a parent and a child. As much as a child loves a parent, a parent will always love a child more, because the parent has given more and therefore loves more.

When we give something to someone else, we are essentially giving that person a piece of ourselves. The more we give, the more we become a part of that other person. Since we naturally love ourselves (or should!), this love will eventually flow to the recipient of our giving. When we give to a neighbor, a stranger, or yes, even a difficult family member, we will see ourselves in them, and that's how we will be able to love them as ourselves.

Try it out. There may already be a challenging person in your life, or you may find a difficult stranger pop into your life, even for just a few moments. Give something to them. It doesn't have to be much — a smile, a compliment, a small favor. As you do, you will see a change take place. The more you give, the more love you will have to give, and consequently, the more love you will receive in return.

Love Your Neighbor: Devotion 3

LIVE AS AN OPEN BOOK

"'IF ANY OF YOUR FELLOW
ISRAELITES BECOME POOR
AND ARE UNABLE TO SUPPORT
THEMSELVES AMONG YOU,
HELP THEM AS YOU WOULD
A FOREIGNER AND STRANGER,
SO THEY CAN CONTINUE
TO LIVE AMONG YOU.'"

— Leviticus 25:35

Judaism's Oral Tradition provides a startling insight into the actions of some of the most righteous figures in the Bible. The Jewish sages claim that if Reuben had known that God would record in the Bible that he had saved Joseph's life, he would have carried Joseph on his own shoulders back to their father, Jacob.

The sages continue and explain that if Aaron had known that it would be recorded by God in the Bible how his heart was joyous and not even a bit jealous when he saw Moses appointed the leader of Israel, he would have gone out to greet Moses with music and dancing.

As a third example, the sages say that if Boaz had known that it would be recorded in the Bible that he gave grain to an impoverished Ruth, he would instead have fed her with fattened cows. The sages conclude: When you do a good deed, do it with all your heart, in the best way possible.

In these verses from Leviticus chapter 25,

we are instructed to help a brother or sister in need. *"If any of your fellow Israelites become poor and are unable to support themselves among you, help them as you would a foreigner and stranger, so they can continue to live among you."* Then the next verse continues with the following stipulation: *"Do not take interest or any profit from them, but fear your God, so that they may continue to live among you."*

Rabbi Yechiel Eckstein distributing blankets with Operation Winter Warmth

It's understandable that the Bible would deter us from profiting off another person's hard times, but we might think that this injunction would be based on *"but love your neighbor like yourself."* What does *"but fear your God"* have to do with it?

Fear of God means living with the awareness that God is watching and recording everything that we do. It says in Malachi: *"Then those who feared the LORD talked with each other, and the LORD listened and heard. A scroll of remembrance was written in his presence concerning those who feared the LORD and honored his name"* (3:16). When we do something, God notices and He records it. So how could we possibly charge the poor man interest or give a loan while making a profit? How could we do any good deed in any way other than our very best?

This week, try to bring *"fear of God"* into your life in a new way. Any time you do something good for someone else, imagine God Himself writing it down. How does that change the way you do things? Live your life like it's an open book — because the truth is, it really is!

Love Your Neighbor: Devotion 4

WHAT ABOUT WE?

DO NOT LET KINDNESS
AND TRUTH LEAVE YOU;
BIND THEM AROUND
YOUR NECK, WRITE
THEM ON THE TABLET
OF YOUR HEART.

— Proverbs 3:3 NASB

There is a story about a Jewish man who wrote a letter to his rabbi because he was unhappy and needed guidance in getting his life on track. The letter read: "I need your help. I wake up every day sad and anxious. I have difficulty concentrating. I find it hard to pray. I feel that life has lost its joy and meaning. I need help." The rabbi delivered his reply without writing a single word. Instead, the rabbi took a red pen and circled the first word of every sentence: "I."

The message was that the solution to the person's problem could be found in his focus exclusively on himself. The rabbi was trying to gently, yet firmly, demonstrate that the secret to a happy and fulfilling life is to not focus on ourselves all the time, but to focus on the needs of others. The happiest people in the world are the ones who make other people happy.

In Proverbs 3:3, we read this powerful message: *"Do not let kindness and truth leave you; Bind them around your neck, Write them on the tablet of your heart."* King Solomon recognized the importance of kindness, too. By telling us to bind it to our necks and inscribe it on our hearts, he was teaching us that we ought to make kindness — as well as truth — a major part of who we are both inside and out.

Most people go through life asking themselves, "What is in it for me?" However, this ultimately leads to a shallow existence and a feeling of emptiness. Life lived "all about me" can be a very lonely experience. Instead of asking "What about me?" we should start asking, "What about we?"

In other words, how can I help others? How can I brighten someone else's day? How can I make the world better for everyone?

The *Talmud* teaches that kindness is even better than charity because it can be done for both poor and rich, and with money or without any. Everyone can perform acts of kindness today. Speak some encouraging words to someone who is down. Cook a hot meal for someone alone or hungry. Help someone run an errand, or offer your seat on the crowded bus to another person. Even something as simple as asking, "What can I do for YOU today" can enrich your life as well as many others.

Make kindness a priority today!

Love Your Neighbor: Devotion 5

LOVING THE UNLOVABLE

ALL OF YOU ARE STANDING TODAY IN THE PRESENCE OF THE LORD YOUR GOD—YOUR LEADERS AND CHIEF MEN, YOUR ELDERS AND OFFICIALS, AND ALL THE OTHER MEN OF ISRAEL, TOGETHER WITH YOUR CHILDREN AND YOUR WIVES, AND THE FOREIGNERS LIVING IN YOUR CAMPS WHO CHOP YOUR WOOD AND CARRY YOUR WATER.

— Deuteronomy 29:10-11

We have all encountered people who seem downright unlovable. It could be the cranky person who never has anything good to say. It could be a nasty salesclerk or a driver who cuts you off in traffic. Our gut instinct is to dislike these people; however, we know that God wants us to behave differently. In Leviticus 19:18, we are commanded to *"love your neighbor as yourself,"* and by *"your neighbor,"* God means everyone, and by *"love,"* God doesn't mean just tolerate.

But how are we to love the unlovable?

Consider these words of Moses to the children of Israel from Deuteronomy chapter 29: *"All of you are standing today in the presence of the LORD your God—your leaders and chief men, your elders and officials, and all the other men of Israel, together with your children and your wives, and the foreigners living*

in your camps who chop your wood and carry your water."

The date was the seventh day of the Hebrew month of *Adar*, the day on which Moses was to die. His purpose on that day was to seal the covenant between God and the children of Israel. The Jewish sages teach that by gathering all the people, from young to old, from the leaders to the water-carriers, Moses was teaching the people that before they could become deserving of God's unconditional love, they had to unconditionally love each other. They needed to stand undivided, loving each person as they did themselves.

The sages teach that the sin that led to the destruction of the Temple, God's dwelling place on earth, was the sin of "baseless hatred." According to Jewish tradition, God said, "If you can't live with each other, I won't live with you." The antidote to the sin of baseless hatred is "baseless

love." When we can embrace each other uncon-ditionally, God will return once again.

Still, we are left with the question of how to love those who are hard to love. I have seen many suggestions and strategies. However, I think they all miss the point. Baseless hatred means that a person hates another person for no reason — just because. And that's exactly how we need to implement baseless love — just because! There is no reason. It may even seem *unreasonable* to love that person. But we love them just because.

We need to stop looking so closely at other people and judging them. We need to remember that there is more to any individual's story than we may know. We need to quit analyzing the behavior of others and just love. When we love others despite their flaws, we will feel God's love for us in spite of our own shortcomings.

Love Your Neighbor: Devotion 6

BUILDING THE WORLD WITH KINDNESS

I WILL DECLARE
THAT YOUR LOVE STANDS
FIRM FOREVER, THAT
YOU HAVE ESTABLISHED
YOUR FAITHFULNESS
IN HEAVEN ITSELF.

— Psalm 89:2

According to Jewish tradition, when God created the world it was teetering like a chair with only three legs until God added a fourth leg — kindness. This idea is alluded to in Psalm 89 when we read, *"I will declare that your love stands firm forever ..."* In Hebrew, the word *olam* can mean "forever" as it is translated here, but it can also mean "world." Following the latter translation, this verse has an alternate meaning that is a well-known maxim in the Jewish tradition. We translate it as, "I will declare — the world is built on kindness."

This idea is true on so many levels. For example, each human being who enters the world is dependent on the kindness of others. As infants, we can't take care of ourselves. We are dependent on  someone to feed us, clean us, and keep us safe from harm. Someone had to go out of their way, and more often than not, give up a lot of sleep, so that we could make it through the first years of life.

 Toward the end of our lives, many of us become just as dependent or at least somewhat dependent upon others. Again, as we age, we need acts of kindness from others to keep healthy physically and to maintain our emotional well-being.

In between the beginning and the end of our lives, we might think that we are independent and not in need of the kindness of others. However, life has a way of teaching us otherwise. We go through challenging times, and we need the people around us to help us out, even if it is just with a word of encouragement or a smile.

People are created with kindness, and that is what it means when our sages teach that the world is built on kindness. We are the world, and we would be nothing without the love and giving of those around us.

Think back to a time when you were in need of kindness and you received it. How did that affect your day and your life? Now think of a time that you really could have used some help, financially, emotionally, or otherwise — but you did not receive it. How did that affect you?

Let's use our memories of kindness — both receiving and not — to motivate us to help others. One small act of kindness can go a long way in the life of another person. Moreover, kindness tends to have a ripple effect as the beneficiaries often pass it along to others. Who knows the impact one act of kindness can have on the world?

Indeed, the world is built on kindness, and we can be a part of building God's world, one kindness at a time.

Love Your Neighbor: Devotion 7

I AM MY BROTHER'S KEEPER

Cain and Abel *by Julius Schnorr von Carolsfeld, Woodcut for "Die Bibel in Bildern", 1860*

THEN THE LORD SAID TO CAIN, "WHERE IS YOUR BROTHER ABEL?" "I DON'T KNOW," HE REPLIED. "AM I MY BROTHER'S KEEPER?"

— Genesis 4:9

A great rabbi once made the following statement: "We must live with the times!" Knowing that the rabbi was not in favor of trading a traditional lifestyle for a more modern way of life, his students asked him what he meant. The rabbi explained: "The *Torah* is God's truth, eternally and universally relevant. By contemplating the weekly *Torah* reading, we can learn how to live spiritually in every situation."

In other words, the rabbi was teaching us that the Bible continues to have a message particularly relevant to our personal lives today.

This teaching always comes back to me when I read about the encounter between God and Cain, just after the murder of Abel. God asked Cain, *"Where is your brother Abel?"* Then came Cain's infamous reply: *"Am I my brother's keeper?"*

The Jewish sages point out that, of course, God knew where Abel was. What He was really asking Cain was, "What have you done to your brother?" God was giving Cain a chance to take responsibility for his actions. However, Cain did the exact opposite. His reply meant, "You, God, are responsible for Abel's death. You alone determine who will live and who will die. I am not responsible."

FIDF Impact Event,
November 11, 2009

Now, although our personal life situations don't mirror Cain's actions, I always feel that the conversation between Cain and God is also happening between us and God, as well. It's as if God is saying to us: "Where are your brothers? Are you aware that people are starving in one country and dying of disease in another? Are you aware that there are hungry children in your town or that there are elderly who are cold because they can't afford heat? What have you done for your brothers?"

God gives us a chance to take responsibility and demonstrate that we are part of the solution, not the problem. So, how do we answer? Do we turn our backs and, like Cain, say, "Am I my brother's keeper?" Or do we accept God's challenge and partnership by proudly declaring, "I am my brother's keeper. And my sister's keeper. And I will help them in any way that I can."

In Isaiah 58, God implores us to stop injustice, free the oppressed, clothe the naked, feed the hungry, and provide shelter for the poor. Consider today how you might do to become the keepers of our brothers and sisters.

Love Your Neighbor: Devotion 8

UNITED IN BROTHERLY LOVE

"'I WILL MAKE THEM ONE NATION IN THE LAND, ON THE MOUNTAINS OF ISRAEL. THERE WILL BE ONE KING OVER ALL OF THEM AND THEY WILL NEVER AGAIN BE TWO NATIONS OR BE DIVIDED INTO TWO KINGDOMS.'"

— Ezekiel 37:22

In Jewish folklore, a story is told about how and why God picked Mount Moriah to be the site of His Holy Temple.

There were once two brothers who lived in two villages and shared the land between them. Every year they would divide the harvest. During one abundant year, the older brother who was married and had many children was worried about his younger brother who didn't have a family. Who would support him in his old age? In the middle of the night, the older brother secretly brought several sheaves of grain to his brother's storehouse, but when he woke up in the morning, he still had exactly the same amount of grain that he had the night before.

The younger brother was also worried: How will my brother support so many children? So, the younger brother decided to secretly travel to his brother's storehouse and place several sheaves of his own inside, but in the morning, he discovered that he still had exactly the same amount of grain as he had before he gave any away.

This went on for two nights until on the third night, the two brothers met each other on the way to the other's storehouse carrying several sheaves of grain. At once, they both understood what had happened and they embraced in brotherly love. At that moment, God decided that the mountain where the two brothers met, Mount Moriah, would be the site of His future home. The love that the brothers had for each other drew God to live among them at that place.

In verses taken from Ezekiel chapter 37, the prophet predicted that while the children of Israel had been split into two kingdoms in ancient times — ten tribes in the Northern Kingdom and Judah and Benjamin in the Southern Kingdom — in the future, the rift would be mended and the two would become one. Just a few verses later, God said through the prophet that He would place His sanctuary among the united people forever (Ezekiel 37:26-28).

The Jewish sages explain that the two prophecies are connected. When there is unity and love among His people, God will dwell among them.

There are many ways to connect with God. We can pray and we can study God's Word. However, the story of the two brothers and the prophecies of Ezekiel point out another important route. When we pour out our love for our brothers and sisters, we draw God's love toward us.

This week, let us make a special effort to connect in a deeper way with someone we know who might be lonely or in need. When we embrace each other, God embraces us in turn.

Love Your Neighbor: Devotion 9
"HOW GOOD AND PLEASANT"

BEHOLD, HOW GOOD
AND HOW PLEASANT IT
IS FOR BRETHREN TO
DWELL TOGETHER
IN UNITY!"
— Psalm 133:1 (NKJV)

In a Peanuts cartoon, Lucy demands that Linus change the TV channel, threatening him with her fist. "What makes you think that you can walk in here and take over?" Linus asks.

"These five fingers," says Lucy. "Individually they're nothing, but when I curl them together like this into a single unit, they form a weapon that is terrible to behold."

Defeated, Linus replies, "Which channel do you want?" Then he looks at his own fingers and says, "Why can't you guys get organized like that?"

Indeed, when things or people come together, they are far more powerful than on their own. Individual snowflakes are powerless, even fragile, but just look at what they can do when they stick together!

Power and strength are not the only positives to come out of unity. When people stick together, we are capable of creating new things and discovering new cures. We can make a better life that all people can enjoy. This is what the psalmist means when he writes, *"How good and pleasant it is for brethren to dwell together in unity."*

It's not just the absence of fighting that makes it *"good and pleasant"* when God's people live together — it's the presence of great innovation and capability that results when people help each other, work and live together, and create a better world.

The Jewish sages point out a very significant change that occurs in the Bible when it describes the children of Israel at Mount Sinai. The verse simply says, *"and Israel camped there in the desert in front of the mountain"* (Exodus 19:2). However, in the original Hebrew, it's easy to recognize that Scripture changes from speaking about the Israelites in the plural tense and instead describes them grammatically as a single unit.

This is because, as the sages explain, when the Israelites were at the foot of Mount Sinai, it was as if they shared "one heart and one soul." They had merged into one unit. It is because of this unity that they merited receiving God's revelation and His law in the Ten Commandments.

If the unity of the Israelites in ancient times could bring God down to earth, imagine what will happen when God's people come together in our times!

Here at *The Fellowship* we celebrate the unity between Jews and Christians who all share the same love for God, the Bible, and Israel. Together we work tirelessly to fulfill God's purposes. Join us in our holy work and together we will see with our own eyes, *"Behold, how good and how pleasant it is for brethren to dwell together in unity!"*

Love Your Neighbor: Devotion 10

"TWO ARE BETTER THAN ONE"

Solomon *by Gustave Doré*

TWO ARE BETTER THAN
ONE, BECAUSE THEY
HAVE A GOOD RETURN
FOR THEIR LABOR.
— Ecclesiastes 4:9

In Ecclesiastes, King Solomon, the wisest of all men, teaches: *"Two are better than one, because they have a good return for their labor."* But is that such a profound idea? Isn't it obvious that two people will accomplish more together than alone?

The truth is that, in practice, we tend to live quite differently. Society has long been based on the notion of competition — that only one of us can succeed; only one of us can have what we all want. However, it's time to shift from competition to a paradigm of collaboration where we all can benefit by helping each other.

Let's take a look at some practical applications to our lives. Solomon mentions four in Ecclesiastes 4:9–12. In verse 9, we learn that there is a better return for our labor, meaning we are more productive when part of a team. Whether it be in the workplace or at home, we are more creative and effective when we can exchange ideas and learn from each other.

Next, Solomon wrote in 4:10 that if one

person falls, the other person can pick up the fallen individual. Again, on the surface, this seems more like common sense than great wisdom. But on a deeper and more spiritual level, this teaches us that when we have a companion or spiritual guide, we have someone to direct us if we fall out of line. We should cultivate such relationships and welcome constructive criticism. It's not always fun to hear, but when someone points out how we might be falling, they can literally save our spiritual lives.

Solomon continued in verse 11, explaining that when two lie down together, they can keep each other warm. Again, this is true on a physical level and instructive on a spiritual level. When going through dark and difficult times, we all need a friend to comfort us and encourage us.

Finally, Solomon taught in verse 12 that while one person could be easily overpowered, two could fight off attackers. This is true of spiritual assaults as well. In the same way we might find a running partner to help us train and ward off laziness, we can also find a friend to help us beat the urge to gossip or keep us accountable to some other spiritual goal.

In so many ways, as Solomon taught, two are better than one. This principle is underscored in the *Talmud* in the following story about a Jewish sage who had been asleep for 70 years. When he finally awoke, he headed straight to the study hall only to discover that all his peers

Young children in Israel

and study partners had already passed away. At that point, he expressed the famous line: "Give me companionship or give me death!" He recognized that he could not live effectively without at least one good companion.

Look for those people, be it friends, partners or mentors to help you through the different challenges in life. Indeed, two are better than one, and we are all better together.